WE NEED TO DO BETTER

D1417032

DR. PAUL MILLER

WE NEED TO DO BETTER

Changing the Mindset of Children through
Family, Community, and Education

CHALFANT ECKERT

PUBLISHING

We Need to Do Better

Copyright © 2016 Dr. Paul Miller. All Rights Reserved.

No rights claimed for public domain material, all rights reserved. No parts of this publication may be reproduced, stored in any retrieval system, or transmitted in any form or by any means, electronic, mechanical, recording, or otherwise, without the prior written permission of the author. Violations may be subject to civil or criminal penalties.

Library of Congress Number: 2016932581

ISBN: 978-1-63308-218-2 (paperback)
      978-1-63308-219-9 (ebook)

Cover and Interior Design by R'tor John D. Maghuyop

CHALFANT ECKERT
PUBLISHING

1028 S Bishop Avenue, Dept. 178
Rolla, MO 65401

Printed in the United States of America

TABLE OF CONTENTS

SECTION 4

EDUCATION IS THE NEW FORM OF CIVIL RIGHTS

SECTION 5

RITUALS AND ROUTINES FOR RUNNING EFFECTIVE SCHOOLS SO CHILDREN DON'T FAIL

INTRODUCTION

Every child should have a chance to succeed in life, but there is an enormous disparity between the *haves* and *have-nots*. The separation between the two is lack of wealth, which doesn't only refer to money. It also includes knowledge. I was listening to Jeezy's new 19-track album, *Church in the Streets* (while I was writing this) and he said, "being rich is a talent and being broke is a profession." (November 2013). He is referred to as a Reverend with street disciples.

Jeezy preaches and teaches in ways that his audience resonates with, and they get his message. My goal with this book is to preach and teach in ways that resonate with my audience and help them get the message. Anyone interested in the dynamics of urban education will find this book interesting, but I aim my writing predominantly toward educators, seeking to inspire them to take a stand against failures and broken mentality. Being broke, being poor, is a mindset that is formulated by one generation and passed down from generation to generation. The cycle can be broken with the great equalizer: Education. It can break the poor mentality and level the playing fields for all stakeholders.

The playing fields cannot be leveled if over half the students in urban cities aren't graduating high school. This is a systemic problem that needs to be addressed, but cannot be done by looking at the educational system in isolation. A holistic approach must be taken and put into action by schools, parents, and communities. WE HAVE TO DO BETTER! We need to all step up and address the low graduation rates as a team. What I will ask throughout this book is that you personally take a stand! I ask you to make a commitment that in the next year of your life you will make it your personal mission to eliminate failures. Do not let any children fail this year.

As an educator, you probably already know that failures in high school are the greatest factors in whether a student will graduate. Many kids don't have a chance to graduate for various reasons. They fail, they drop out, and the cycle continues. We have to work together to make the cycle stop.

We can come up with many reasons a child might drop out: poverty and the poor living conditions that come with it, inadequate education systems for low-income school districts and the students they serve, poor community resources and support and lack of knowledge about how to access those resources, and family units without proper supervision and encouragement. These are in no particular order, but all have the potential to make failure a popular choice. In this book, I will address the implications of all these causes, and suggest potential actions that educational systems, leaders, teachers, parents, and students can take to improve the situation.

What if our country with its communities, parents, and concerned citizens decided to stand up and do something about our children failing and falling through the cracks? Together we could make a difference in the lives of thousands of young people, even though the cracks are so big that research suggests large urban cities have a disparaging deficit of students graduating. The New York Times reports that only 53% of students in urban areas graduate compared to 70% for their suburban counterpart.

I am realistic, and I know that it would take more than a year to solve urban educational failures, but we must start somewhere. What I am proposing is that this book is used as a starting point, a beginning for breathing life into an enormous problem which has only been regulated with more rigorous standards, but not corrected, by the government agencies that increasing those standards.

The *2012 Schott Report* likens it to throwing a child who can't swim into deep ocean waters. Once they are in and get close to the orange marker, someone moves it further away. Wouldn't it be smarter to throw the child a lifeline? What the hell, maybe we could just jump in and swim with the child to safety. Maybe it is time we take the leap of faith and delve passionately into the deep end of the pool of the educational problem of failures in our society and rescue the people drowning in it, our kids. The time to act is now.

WE CAN STOP KIDS FROM FAILING!

1

SECTION

BACKGROUND
WHO AM I AND WHY SHOULD MY VOICE MATTER?

HOW I GREW UP

I am technically Black, Hispanic, and White. My maternal grandparents are White and their ethnic background combined German, Russian, Italian, and Spanish, but if asked, they say they are Jewish. My grandparents taught me early on that in different settings, I had to conduct myself in different ways. While I was with my grandparents I had to behave properly or in slang terms, I had to "act White." When I was home or at school, if I would have acted White, I would have been picked on and never heard the end of it.

Although my mother tried to be there for me during my formative years, she had her own struggles and was emotionally absent, so my grandparents filled the void and helped to lay a strong foundation for my growth and development. They never went to college, but regretted it and felt that they had to work harder because of it. My grandfather was a car salesman, and my grandmother was a legal secretary.

My grandfather took me fishing, swimming, and golfing, and my grandmother made sure that I had a hot meal when we came home. We ate dinner together as a family, and they often asked me how my day at school had been. My grandmother always said, "If you want to have a good life, you have to go to college and make something of yourself." I listened intently until it became deeply ingrained in my spirit as a belief that would guide the rest of my life. The value of school was deeply planted in my psyche, and I was able to call on it in times of need to give me the extra motivation to succeed.

My mother who was raised by my grandparents as well always felt like she was trapped in the wrong culture. She didn't identify with any of her parents' beliefs. She intentionally sabotaged everything they tried to instill in her. She wanted to be opposite and was embarrassed to be affiliated with any of their belief about school and work. To her credit, she inherited strong morals, which I believe was transferred to me as well. In her teenage years, Mom was rebellious; she was brilliantly smart but hung with people who acted stupidly. She wanted to be around the tough guys, the "hoods," people who smoked a lot, didn't value education, and only valued having a good time.

Mom barely made it through high school and came to the conclusion that college was for "lames." My grandparents' did everything they could to help her, but she strayed ever further away from their beliefs.

In the mid-1970's my mother met my father. My father is Puerto Rican and Black. His grandmother was a slave from Africa, but if asked my relatives on that side of the family only identified with being Puerto Rican. I was born in 1978, raised by a single mother - my father was an absent dad. During my childhood, my mother was a hairdresser, had several long term relationships at different times, but the longest one was abusive.

When I was eleven years old, we hit hard times. Mom experienced financial woes, so we had to move into The Projects (subsidized housing). There were a lot of houses close together filled with many individuals who faced similar low socioeconomic struggles, trials, and tribulations. It was a place where people bonded because of their similar living conditions. The Projects weren't all fun and games, and danger was obvious. We had Dosha, the mother figure of The Projects who always tried to help. On one occasion, a teenager named Virgil, who lived with his mom next door to Dosha, had about thirty people with weapons come looking for him to beat him up. Dosha was able to convince the mob to leave. Dosha was my Godmother and cousin through my sister's family (you got to be from the hood to understand this one). The Projects were not safe, but they always felt like home to me. When we moved there, I always felt safe because everyone knew me and my mom.

In The Projects, the community looked after its own. We were so poor that there were times we took bottles back to get the deposit so we could buy toilet paper. I remember being embarrassed to go to the store with food stamps. I used to wait outside the store until everyone left out before buying whatever my mother sent me to get. All us kids were embarrassed to use food stamps, but we all had them. We just didn't want to be the brunt of jokes from kids who didn't need food stamps, so we just didn't talk about them. My mother had my sister, and I became her surrogate dad at twelve years old because I was the man of the house. I wanted to be a good example for her, and that is part of the reason I worked so hard. I wanted her to be proud of me and aspire to be like me. Having a little sister forced me to grow up. I was often left in charge because my mother was depressed over Jerome (her drug-addicted boyfriend who fathered my sister).

I could always hear in my grandparents' voices that school was important and that it was my ticket out of the life I lived with my mother. The experiences growing up in the hood with my mom in less than privileged circumstances made me a strong man who never gives up, and I learned a lot from watching her mistakes. I love her for it and have seen her grow light years since my youth.

As I approached my teenage years, my friends became my family. We did everything together and taught each other how to be men. Most of us did not have our fathers, so we were role models for each other. The neighborhood raised me and helped me become a man. Adult supervision didn't provide much guidance, so some decisions I made could have resulted in jail time. I was lucky to make it and developed into a successful man, a Black (biracial man). By age thirteen, I considered myself a Black man, which is who I was, and I was comfortable with that choice.

I could have chosen to go down a path that would lead to a life of prison, and I did participate in a few activities that definitely could have resulted in that lifestyle. I made some poor life choices, but I was able to turn the corner and go a different direction to get to where I am now. When times got tough, and I thought about breaking the law and doing things that could cause me to lose my freedom, I retreated to my foundational values instilled in me about school by my grandparents. Each time the streets could have drowned me, I swam to safety by getting an education. It wasn't always easy because living in The Projects surrounded me with opportunities to participate in illegal activities.

There were abundant opportunities to make bad choices. My friend's brother moved into the house next door occupied by a woman addicted to crack. He had a relationship with her daughter, and he started to sell crack out of the house. I witnessed this friend and many others I knew start selling drugs. People from The Manor would come around in their fancy cars with lots of jewelry acquired from selling drugs. My friends and I saw them and wanted those material things for ourselves. Most of the material wealth of The Projects came from selling drugs, commonly referred to as *hustling*. It was fast and easy money, but I decided to work for mine.

I got a paper route, then pushed carts for Wegmans (the best grocery store ever), then got a job selling clothes in a clothing store in downtown Rochester. I worked, went to school, and played football. I tried hard to do the right thing, but it seemed like no matter what I did, I was always still broke. I was tired of being broke, so I resorted to different forms of hustling to make extra money. It didn't last long because I kept imagining the disappointment my grandparents would feel if I got caught. I could also hear my mother telling me that God had a plan for me, and that is not it.

The thought of disappointing my grandparents scared me. My friends were not worried what their parents thought, some of their parents supported the notion of having extra income in the household regardless of how it was obtained. Needless to say, I stopped hustling and continued working and going to school.

Along this teenage path, I had a few role models who helped me see what a "Good Black Man" looked like. I might not have been successful if a few positive Black role models had not modeled appropriate behaviors. One of the few role models was Tony Jordan. He had played professional football and at the time, was home with a knee injury. He became active in the community and gave of his time to young men, teaching us about college life and life skills. Another influential man was Ken Mangrum, a family man. He was in charge of a group called *The Kappa League*. His fraternity started a group that gave back to high school boys in the community. He would pick us up every Friday night and take us to do something special. We might play basketball, hang at his house, and he even took me on a trip to Detroit. He reinforced family values, and he instilled in me the importance of giving back to your community. I learned that lesson, and I later became a member of *THE Omega Psi Phi Fraternity Inc.* — Greeks will understand this one – RQQ - Bruhz.

The only other positive role model I had was my high school football coach. I was ready to quit playing football, and he took the time to talk to me. He said in his gruff voice, "God Dam it son, you better not give up, you are a good football player, you could be better if you played with some God damn fire. Stop pussyfooting around." He actually called me more than that and said worse, but I don't want anyone to negatively criticize someone who really molded my thought process through a much-needed cuss out. Those few sentences turned me into a beast; they motivated me and helped me to become a real player and a real man. I never forgot his words; I took them with me to the college football field, school, life, and basically everywhere I go.

These role models helped me to realize that I wanted to pursue a career in education so I could work with children and give back as well. The circumstances of my growing up, the situation in the hood, and the desire to help children in the same circumstances inspired my lifelong career as an educator.

Students (especially students of color) must be determined and resolute to fight their circumstances. They have to make right decisions and get an education to make life better for themselves and get out of the Projects. It takes concentrated effort to succeed so they can influence society and give back to the community. To make success possible and easier, educators need to step in and organize programs that provide suitable mentors for the students of color. Educators should take a special interest in students, make strict rules to guide them and encourage them to take their education seriously and help them avoid distractions, so they graduate high school.

PROFESSIONAL JOURNEY

I started teaching and coaching at age 22. I was motivated to make a difference because I had grown up in The Projects and had lived in undesirable circumstances, and understood the need for education and mentoring. I knew I was doing what God wanted me to do. God is my light and Savior, and I know that by following His path, I will always be successful.

It is my destiny to touch the lives of young people and help them to be better people. I enjoyed teaching, but I loved coaching. I could get to know people and their personalities on a personal level, and instill good morals and values in them. All of my previous life experiences have helped me to reach back and pull students forward. I use my past struggles and experiences to help students see that they can succeed if they make opportunities for themselves and refuse to give up.

I attended School without Walls High School in Rochester, New York, and after graduating in 1996, went on to college. I completed the teacher certification program earned my Bachelor of Science degree in Physical Education, and completed my Master's coursework in Physical Education Athletic Administration from State University of New York at Brockport. After graduation, I was hired as Assistant Principal at a local high school. I initially became an administrator in the Rochester City School District (RCSD) because I did not like the way other administrators were running their schools. I felt like I could do it better, so I went back to college to learn how. I attended St. John Fisher College in Rochester where I earned a Master's degree in Educational Administration and an Educational Doctorate in Executive Leadership.

I have over fifteen years' experience in urban public education systems specializing in school redesign and reform by creating effective change for schools through collaborative missions, visions, and teamwork. In the past fifteen years of administrative experience, I have held many billets including Chief Executive Officer (CEO) and Principal of a charter school, Assistant Principal of a Small Learning Community, worked in operations/safety/security, and been a summer school Principal. I also have six years of executive experience as Director of Operations for Team E Foundation, a not-for-profit organization. I was instrumental in its growth and development into a nationally recognized organization.

I have been successful at operating and organizing all aspects of one of the nation's largest cash-paying Street Basketball tournaments, which raises funds to provide full-tuition scholarships for inner city youth who deserve a second chance.

I have been privileged to be recognized by and receive several nominations from various prestigious organizations. Recently, I was nominated to join and accepted by the Southern Christian Leadership Conference (SCLC), an international civil rights organization, as a council member for the Next Generation Leadership Council. I will be working to improve youth issues in the United States and internationally.

In 2015, I was recognized by Israel AME Church as their Men of Honor "Man of the Year." I was also nominated by Congressional Hispanic Caucus Institute (CHCI) as one of the Top 20 Educators in the Country and received Distinguished Leadership Awards from St. John Fisher College and Kappa Alpha Psi.

In 2012, I was recognized by the City and the County of Albany as a *Man of Valor* and as one of the *40 Under 40 Top African American Leaders* in Rochester in 2011.

Rochester Business Journal acknowledged me as "Talent on the Move." In 2005, I was awarded the *Who's Who Among Students in American Universities and Colleges*. Additionally, I have been privileged to make appearances for local news stations and colleges, and as an expert guest panelist in Black females' experiences with cyberbullying. In addition, I assisted in the writing of *The Cyberbullying Manual* with Dr. Jim Colt and Dr. Sam McQuade. Recently, I authored my first book called *Cyberbullying: Breaking the Cycle of Conflict*.

I have run Green Tech High Charter School in Albany, New York for the past four school years with stellar results, more than doubling the graduation rates for Black males recognized by the State of New York. The school has 97% black males and over 80% of them live at or below the poverty line, yet we have had over an 80% graduation rate every year I have been in charge. Last year we had a 91% graduation rate, 100% acceptance to 2- or 4-year college (59% 4 year), and over $4.5 million in scholarships.

We have made great strides in the school, and a prime example is scholarship awards. In 2012, we had $20,000. That grew to $300,000 in 2013, $1.5 million in 2014, and $4.5 million in 2015. In addition, we built a State Championship Class AA Basketball program which was a resounding success. Green Tech High Charter School is one of the best high schools in New York state, with all seniors graduating and being accepted into college. The future looks promising for Green Tech students and the Albany, New York community.

My biggest professional accomplishments are when students graduate and walk across the stage towards an adult life filled with potential success unhindered by societal woes because they have an education. I take immense pride in knowing I played a part in their lives and began a cycle of paying it forward for future generations. The best feelings are when students who may not have previously seen the light at the end of the tunnel wake up and become not only productive but also willing to help others become productive.

I hope that my journey from the dangerous housing projects of Rochester to become an impactful educator inspire and help others to accept their own destiny; this is why I chose to be an administrator in schools. I strive to be a positive role model and an agent of change.

From years of experience and antecedents as an administrator, it is evident that I have built systems that are the reason why we don't fail.

WHERE I AM NOW AND WHY YOU SHOULD CARE

(Because together, we can keep kids from failing!)

I came from The Projects in one of the worse cities in America. Rochester, New York is currently the fifth poorest city, has the highest murder rate per capita in the state, very often has murder rates that are in top 10 overall in the country, and has the lowest graduation rates for black males at 9% in 2012. In spite of my unfortunate circumstances, I fought against all odds to get out of the ghetto and become an adult that touches lives and impacts communities positively. My journey through diverse experiences and trying to figure out my identity has led me to leadership roles within the school system. Early on, my lack of identity limited my confidence as a person, especially in social settings. To truly learn who I was as a person and to become comfortable with who I was, I had to accept my journey. Accepting my journey and learning from my peers and role models helped me to have the confidence I need to be successful today.

As a teacher and a coach, I was able to work with young people on a different level. My experiences as a teacher and coach also helped me to grow and mature into a better person. It has given me eternal youth, but a level a maturity that ensures professionalism. Becoming an educator has also steered my personal life. If I had not pursued education, I might be involved in illegal activities as many of my lifelong friends still are. I could not have left The Projects if not for education.

Public Broadcasting System (2014) reported statistics in the Tavis Smiley *Outcomes for Young Black Men Fact Sheet* that showed a predominantly high rate of failure among students of color and disparity in achievement gaps between Black and other races:

- 54% of African Americans graduate from high school, compared to more than three-quarters of White and Asian students.
- Nationally, African American male students in grades K-12 were nearly 2½ times as likely to be suspended from school in 2000 as White students.
- In 2007, nearly 6.2 million young people were high school dropouts. Every student who does not complete high school costs our society an estimated $260,000 in lost earnings, taxes, and productivity.
- On average, African American twelfth-grade students read at the same level as White eighth-grade students.
- The twelfth-grade reading scores of African American males were significantly lower than those for men and women across every other racial and ethnic group.

We need to take a stand and stop allowing our children of color to fail. I believe my voice matters because I'm a person of authority by virtue of experience and success as an educator in building education systems that do not fail. It is important to build school policies that work.

Green Tech High Charter School with 97% Black male students has impressive graduation rates (91% last year) when compared to New York state's 37% graduation rate for Black males (Schott Foundation, 2012). I created a program loosely based on a program I witnessed in Tennessee while on a professional development visit. I took what I learned back to my current building and collaboratively devised a way to make the program our own. The program is called RAZE UP. The RAZE stands for Remove All Zeroes Effectively. The intervention takes place during the school day and 100% of the school body can participate. Data has shown is that it can work for 100% of the student body, but year after year only about 62% take advantage of the intervention. The other 38% either don't do what they are supposed to or fight against it and do nothing at all.

The 62% of the students who actively participate have seen their grades go up four points a week per class in which they were "RAZED" to. Four points a week is statistically significant and has a huge impact on student's bottom line. Basically, what RAZE UP does is create opportunities to make sure that students cannot fail, will not fail, if they care just a tiny bit. What I have done, along with a partner from the school, is create a system and software that assures students won't fail if the school can effectively roll out the system for them.

RAZE UP is further proof that with the right educational system, policies, and high level of support in place, educators can improve the quality of high school educational offerings and rates of student success. Educators bear the responsibility of providing good educational systems that enable better academic performance of children, especially children of color.

THIS YEAR NO CHILD FAILS!!!

The housing projects where I grew up were characterized by low incomes, excessive poverty, high crime, and disproportionate concentrations of minorities such as people of color.

Studies and experience consistently show that public housing developments are located in economically and socially disadvantaged neighborhoods. It is evident that families in projects are less satisfied with their housing, neighborhoods, and schools than other families. Their children are less likely to participate in any extra-curricular activities, are more likely to have changed schools, and are somewhat more likely to have been held back (i.e. had poor academic performance and stunted educational development). Academic performance in early grades has been shown to be a significant predictor of eventual high-school completion, which in turn is linked to future employment probabilities and earnings. It is important to keep students from failing because their lives - and chances of success - are powerfully shaped by the education they receive. Children of color are especially vulnerable to the outcomes of poor educational opportunities and academic failure. Therefore, educators must work towards keeping this group of children from failing. It behooves policy makers and administrators to put improved educational structures and policies in place that lead to improvement in academic performance. Educators should take an in-depth appraisal of existing school policies. It may be that additional resources or different services than otherwise similar schools are needed.

As educators and school administrators we must not fail in our duty to build educational systems that are beneficial and enable kids to succeed.

WE HAVE TO DO BETTER!!

2
SECTION

WHY ARE WE FAILING?

THE CURSE OF WILLIE LYNCH AND ITS SYSTEMIC EFFECTS ON THE BLACK FAMILY STRUCTURE

The year was 1646. The American Commonwealth of Virginia was a colony, a British protectorate in its infancy. The Transatlantic slave trade was in full bloom and thriving. Occasionally, slave ships arrived on New York shores to off-load human cargo. The dark days of slavery were far from over; there was no light on the horizon, except the faint hope of deliverance. The captured prisoners of war from Africa awaited their fate, the terrible fate of slavery!

Upon arrival, many slave masters stood in line to bid. After shaking hands for an executed business deal, they transported their new gains to their plantations. Life on the plantation was anything but peaceful. It was often plagued by uprisings and violence. The children of Africa may have been taken from their natural habitat against their wishes, but by no means was their fighting spirit shattered. Some of them figured out how to escape. Others resorted to violence. Many slave owners were brutally murdered until Willie Lynch, a slave owner himself, came calling.

In 1712, Willie Lynch arrived in the then-colony of Virginia from the West Indies. He came there to teach his methods to the other slave owners. Below is an excerpt from his speech:

"Gentlemen, I have here in my bag a full proof method for controlling your Black slaves. This method, if installed correctly, will control the slaves for at least three hundred years. My method is simple! I have noticed a number of differences among the slaves. Differences in age, intelligence, size and sex. I take these differences and make them bigger! In other words, I use their differences to pitch them against each other. By doing so, the slaves themselves will remain perpetually in cooperative with one another. They will continue to pull each other down to our advantage. This method has worked on my modest plantation in the West Indies!

Now that you have a list of differences, I shall give you an outline of action. But before that, I shall assure you that distrust is stronger than trust and envy stronger than adulation, respect or admiration. I use fear, distrust and envy for control purposes! The Black slaves, after receiving this indoctrination, shall carry on and will become self-refueling and self-generating for hundreds of years. In other words, the niggers would remain envious, distrustful and fearful of each other for generations to come. They would never see eye to eye on anything, let alone unite."

Willie Lynch then proceeded to lecture his audience on how Blacks could remain in a perpetual state of dependency. This is a section of his speech:

"The uncivilized female nigger has a tendency to depend on the uncivilized male nigger for protection. This by nature's design! However, her natural tendency can be reversed, and we did. We reversed nature by burning and pulling a civilized nigger apart and bull whipping the other to the point of death, all in her presence. By her being left alone unprotected, with the protective male image destroyed, the ordeal caused her to move from her psychologically dependent state to a frozen dependent state.

In this frozen psychological state of independence, she will raise her male and female offspring in reversed roles. For fear of the young male's life, she will psychologically train him to be mentally weak and dependent, but physically strong. She will also train her female offspring to be psychologically independent, just like herself. What have you got? You've got the nigger woman out front, the nigger man behind and scared."

There have been suggestions from several quarters that the Willie lynch speech was a hoax. However, the objectives of the methods in this speech were to break the black male, make the female dependent, and the male offspring strong physically but mentally and psychologically weak, sow discord in black communities and distrust in authority. All these characteristics are still evident in the lives of African Americans even in the 21st Century, decades after emancipation. This is one result of the overarching effects of the slave psychology. The slave psychology is such that it breaks the mind and leaves the body intact.

"You cannot get them to work in this natural state. Hence, both the horse and the nigger must be broken; that is breaking them from one form of mental life to another. Keep the body take the mind! In other words, break the will to resist."

–Willie Lynch

Even generations after the end of the slave trade, too many Blacks have maintained a broken mentality as a result of the slave psychology referred to as the *Willie Lynch Curse*. The average Black man (too many of us are okay with AVERAGE), albeit schooled and physically strong, is mentally weak, fearful and lacks creativity.

This broken mentality includes a perpetual lack of value towards education by Blacks. Apathy towards education is more common among the Black race than other races. This is a symptom of the "take the mind keep the body" part of Willie Lynch's speech.

There is also an ingrained and deep level of mistrust for the criminal justice system and authority. African Americans tend to have a higher propensity towards crime and violence than other races, and may be due to our current mindset. Hence, we see a significant number of Blacks having run-ins with the law. Blacks are involved in diverse crimes including riots, arson, murder, gang wars, rape, and armed robbery, etc. The majority of the 2.3 million people incarcerated in U.S. prisons and jails are people of color, people with mental health issues and drug addiction, people with low levels of educational attainment, and people with a history of unemployment or underemployment. We are the minority race and yet have the largest number inmates in our jails (although some are innocent), and most of the crimes are committed against our own people. In addition, parole violations, even among Black male celebrities, are high. Some legal problems can be attributed to the rules and laws which are not designed for Black people. The legal systems can still arguably be called institutionally racist, but our mindsets need to improve to break the cycle that the curse has caused.

Another attribute of the Willie Lynch curse is the generational poverty. Partly due to the apathy towards education, a significant percentage of the black population in the United States is struggling with poverty and deplorable standards of living. High school graduates earn approximately $260,000 more than dropouts (Schott Foundation, 2012). In addition, housing projects serve Black households at a rate substantially greater than their share of the renter population. Forty-eight percent of public housing households are Black compared to only 19% of all renter households.

The Willie Lynch curse is such that the male was disempowered so he could not protect his family. Willie Lynch had an ingenious plan to separate the male and female slaves, and his plan is still effective in many ways today. Hence, Black communities are characterized by broken family structures and pervasive mentalities that failure is acceptable.

"Take two female niggers, one has a boy and the other a female. She will teach the female to be independent because there is no male protector. The other female will teach her son to be dependent, strong but dumb to save his life thereby reversing the natural order of things."

This unnatural order caused the breakdown in African American homes in many ways including a lack of respect for each other, women having babies with no fathers in the home, and Black men abandoning their homes. The goal was never to allow the two sexes to realize that a Black man is designed and fully capable of loving a Black woman unconditionally, and a Black woman is designed to respect a Black man. Consequently, there are broken homes everywhere; single moms, absent dads (males) shirking their responsibilities and not taking care of their families. Kids are growing up without knowing who their fathers are, and in some instances, women have several children fathered by different men.

Black women are over-sexualized as seen in Hip Hop culture, music, and videos. They are seen more as mere sexual objects than they are for their intellectual capacity or what they can offer to society. It's a pathetic situation.

Blacks still possess a distrustful and destructive mindset towards each other. It is imperative that this way of thinking among Blacks is addressed and reversed. We tend to place the blame on Whites for racism, but there is a problem bedeviling us that we cause ourselves. Whites may have been responsible for slavery and for conditioning Blacks to have a slave-like mentality, but it is time to break that mentality for the good of society. It's essential that parents and schools start working to reprogram our children's thoughts. We should start from birth and continue throughout their early childhood education.

> *"The human mind can be rebuilt and restored, and its very essence can be seen and felt. When the mind awakens, the spirit takes over."*
> –Alvin Morrow

Societal rot in the Black community has gone on for too long, and it is high time we African Americans stand up to our responsibilities to ourselves and unborn generations; it's time to free ourselves from mental slavery and shackles. It is time we realize that failure should not be an option; it's time to unite our communities, and time to embrace education and the diverse opportunities it offers. My brothers and sisters let us rise up and fight this demon in our minds constructed by this curse and rid ourselves and our neighborhoods and schools of drugs abuse, violence, murder, and all other vices. We can be free, and that freedom comes from our inner selves. When we unite and rid ourselves of the slave mentality, then we can know that we have freed our race from the Willie Lynch Curse. **We owe it to our unborn generations!**

COMMUNITY

We continuously let down our youth. Social media, TV and music stars have more influence than teachers, doctors, and politicians. Yet the message that continuously flows from us to our children is one that values sex, drugs, no snitching, and Keeping it Real. We say we want what's best, but our actions show different.

When do we start taking responsibility?

Too many parents have failed pass down good morals and societal values to their children. We place emphasis on material wealth and acquisition of possessions rather than moral authority, integrity, and close relationships. Because we often go without the possessions we desire, we place more value on tangible items than intangible character. Our children get caught up in get-rich-quick actions, drug sales, illegal behavior, and schemes to attain fame and fortune. Everyone wants to be a rapper or sports star. We desire the 'bling bling' (shiny) lifestyle without realizing how hard the sports star and the rapper have to work. In the 21st century, the impact of celebrity culture on society, especially on young people is more pronounced than in past generations. Young people are easily influenced by celebrities, sportsmen, actors and actresses, performers, and musicians. In addition, media content has failed children. The influence of the media on the psychosocial development of children is profound. Studies by behavioral experts have shown that children are easily influenced by their environment, and much of what they see and hear only adds to the curse.

Psychologist Albert Bandura's early research in 1965 revealed that children's aggressive acts were partly influenced by what they observed. In general, the more aggressive the people or films that children observe, the more aggressive they act. Learning by watching and imitating others, rather than through one's own personal experiences, is called social learning. According to American Psychological Association, decades of social science research has shown that because violence is mostly a learned behavior, non-violence can also be learned. Psychologists have recently applied these findings towards teaching non-violence to young children and their caregivers. Albert Bandura in one of his early research showed that children's aggressive acts were partly influenced by what they observed (Bandura, 1965) as such since violence is learned, nonviolent ways of interacting with the world can also be learned

'Gangsta rap' is a subgenre of hip-hop music predominantly performed by Blacks and can be associated with street gangs and the "thug" lifestyle. It features lyrics that tells stories of their lives growing up in the hood, hustling, and contains common themes including crime, violence, objectifying women, and drug abuse. The youth and children tend to look up to popular figures in the entertainment world, even if they are not proper role models by virtue of their lifestyles and beliefs. What those kids may not know is that the actual lives of Gangsta Rappers may be totally different from the content and context portrayed in their music. Gangsta Rap contributes to a distinct lack of values, morals, and positive culture, and permeates the strata of too many urban communities.

Children are attracted to the allure and luxury in music videos and movies. They admire entertainment stars, and they want to live the kind of lives portrayed on television, perhaps because kids think it has more sizzle and excitement than pursuing other professions such as in the fields of education, medicine, politics, law, and science. The pull to fame and fortune without effort is strong, and systematically produces a lack of motivation to get an education and live better lives as a result of individual academic efforts. Most young people know that education is important but focus on short-term goals rather than long-term achievement to improve their lives for decades to come. School is just not as attractive or sexy because it does not provide immediate gratification. Career preparation, whether through college or learning a trade, takes years to master and complete.

Children and youth are tempted to explore shortcuts to riches by committing crimes such as dealing in drugs, prostitution, bootlegging, and smuggling, at the expense of their education. They are influenced by their environment and random inputs in such a way as to detect or create patterns of thinking that can be described as inductive learning. The hip hop culture favors Hustlin', showing off, and materialism, hence people's values and morals develop around these aspects and become the dominant culture and mindset. Often the curse of Willie Lynch is perpetuated through our music, entertainment, and mindsets.

Women, specifically Black women are sexualized in music lyrics and videos that portray women as sex toys that have no value other than the pleasure they can offer via intercourse. To buttress this assertation, studies show that up to 75% of videos contain sexually explicit material, and more than half contain violence that is often committed against women. Women are frequently portrayed in a condescending manner that affects children's attitudes about sex roles. Music videos may also reinforce false stereotypes. Sexually aggressive song lyrics influence people to engage in aggressive thoughts, emotions, and behaviors toward the same and the opposite sex. Male participants who heard misogynous song lyrics recalled more negative attributes of women and reported more feelings of vengeance than when they heard neutral song lyrics. In addition, men-hating song lyrics had a similar effect on aggression-related responses of female participants toward men. (Peter Fischer et al., 2006)

The internet is pervasive, everybody has a cell phone, social media site popularity is ever-growing, and television has increased the reach and influence of music lyrics and movies. Role models are unconsciously or consciously exposing children to negative influences to make a dollar. Thus, it is important that parents individually and communities collectively act and limit their children's exposure to media and provide guidance on the age-appropriate use of all media, including television, radio, music, video games, and the internet. Parents must also teach their children the difference between reality and entertainment.

"Freedom means different things in different cultures. For the North American slaveholder freedom means building, raiding, taking over companies, and destroying anyone who gets in the way. For the African American freedom means creativity, the master of one's own destiny in serving the greater good of society. Words have power and when used to control the mind the prevailing thought rules. This is why the media is such a powerful tool. True wealth comes from understanding wealth in producing and marketing not in buying. Constantly buying is an illusion of wealth and classism."
–Alvin Morrow

The bad influence and morality issues are beyond the scope of music lyrics, movies, and social media. However, the influence can be reduced by education, the Black communities have to start ingraining in kids, youth, and adult that whatever is morally wrong is improper, standards have to improve, and people have to respect each other and themselves more. Parents should spend more quality time with their children. And teach them strong moral values via words and actions. Many households teach good values, but more needs to be done in order to make a change. I know this may be controversial and hard to hear, but families need to take a step back and see the truth in this so change can be made.

Media houses can also help out by promoting more shows that reward intelligence, brilliance, and entrepreneurship instead of majorly involving in talent, music and reality shows. Entertainment stars should endeavor to act and use their art in such ways that can be of positive influence to kids that look up to them. African-American entertainers, celebs, and leaders should also be socially responsible by using their leadership positions to positively influence youth.

It is time to break social norms!! In order for us to get the best out of life, we have to change our actions and thought processes. The change has to start from our mindsets; the Black community must deem it fit and prioritize passing good morals, message and values to the younger ones via teaching and their general actions. There should be less emphasis on material wealth and acquisitions of possession, and children should be encouraged to appreciate the value of getting an education.

MISPLACED PRIORITIES BY EDUCATIONAL STAKEHOLDERS

"Education is for improving the lives of others and for leaving your community and world better than you found it."

–Marian Wright Edelman, Founder,
and President of *The Children's Defense Fund.*

We as a people need to take advantage of education. There are higher dropout rates and lower academic performance levels among Blacks in the USA than other races, and poverty levels are higher. A major contributing factor to this problem is the general apathy toward education as too many urban households in poverty place education lower on the totem pole of life's priorities. Although many of these families give lip service to education, their actions do not match their words, and actions send a more powerful message. So let's take a look at why students are failing.

Why are students failing? There are a number of contributing factors, among them, the "unseriousness" of students, flaws of the educational system, inadequate resources, and apathy towards education. There are other root causes that make the reality of a good education for those in poverty seem more like a nightmare than the American dream. Many educators feel powerless to address these bigger issues and are not doing enough to bring solutions because they don't know what to do to bring about lasting change. Teachers and administrators must be willing to address the hard issue of classism in our schools and classrooms. Are you willing?

Classism, as defined by Merriam-Webster (2016) as unfair treatment of people because of their social or economic class, is widespread and well documented. For example, compared with their wealthier peers, poor students are more likely to attend public schools with lesser funding, lower teacher salaries, limited computer and Internet access, larger class sizes, higher student-to-teacher ratios, a less-rigorous curriculum, and fewer experienced teachers. The educational system is inadequate and ineffective in creating positive, sustainable outcomes for these young people stuck in classism while research has consistently shown that support for students is critical to long-term success. At Green Tech, we provide the kinds of support and have implemented reforms that work for students living in low socioeconomic status. Our leaders were willing to change and adjust, and that is what it takes for reform to be effective.

Public schools have and are failing to properly educate African American students— which can be attributed largely to the policies and priorities of the districts. In America's public high schools, 45% of Black students as compared to 22% of whites drop out before their classes graduate. Dropout rates are especially high in urban areas with large minority populations, including such academic basket cases as the District of Columbia (57%), Trenton (59%), Camden (61.4%), Baltimore (65.4%), Cleveland (65.9%), and Detroit (75.1%). Of those Black and Hispanic students who do manage to earn a diploma, large percentages are functionally illiterate. Black high school graduates perform, on average, four academic years below that of their white counterparts. Of all graduates in the Class of 2011, only 11% of Blacks and 15% of Hispanics were proficient in math, as compared to 42% of Whites. Similarly, just 13% of Blacks and 4% of Hispanics were proficient in reading versus 40% of Whites.

Clearly, dismal academic failure is not a problem that can be solved by merely throwing money at it. We have to change the bureaucracy involved in the education sector. Many stakeholders in the education sector (educators and education policymakers) seem to have misplaced priorities and are more concerned about tests and contracts than failing children and implementing the steps needed to keep these kids from drowning in a sea of apathy and inadequate educational preparation for life.

The National Education Association (NEA) has 3.2 million members, and the American Federation of Teachers (AFT) has 1.5 million members. You would think that with 4.7 million educational professions, they could accomplish more than their devotion to promoting political agendas. The NEA derives most of its operating funds from the member dues that, in almost every U.S. state, are deducted automatically from teachers' salaries. Because member dues constitute the very lifeblood of the teachers unions, the unions have made it enormously expensive and time-consuming to get a tenured teacher fired for incompetence. In New York City, for instance, as stated in a report by www.teachersunionexposed, the process of eliminating a single bad teacher costs taxpayers an average of $163,142. In New York State overall, the average is $128,941. Ultimately, the unions strive to keep as many teachers as possible on the payroll— including those who are ineffective—so they can continue to collect their union dues which, in turn, can be applied to political ends. Even in school districts where students perform far below the academic norm for their grade levels, and where dropout rates are astronomically high, scarcely one in a thousand teachers is ever dismissed in any given year

In most states, teachers are automatically awarded tenure after only a few years on the job. *The Los Angeles Times* (December 20, 2009), reported that fewer than 2% of that city's school teachers are denied tenure during the two-year probationary period after they are hired. Once tenured, even the most ineffective and incompetent instructors can have long and relatively lucrative careers in the classroom if they wish to stay in the field of education.

The teachers unions' selfish priorities made bold headlines in 2010, when it was reported that New York City had established a number of so-called "rubber rooms," formally called Temporary Reassignment Centers, where hundreds of public school teachers who had been accused of gross incompetence or misconduct sat idly each day, drawing their full salaries (and thus paying their full union dues) while waiting for their cases to be reviewed. The city not only spent between $35 million and $65 million annually on their salaries and benefits, but also had to bear the additional costs of hiring substitutes to teach the classes that had once been taught by the idle instructors, and renting space wherein the reassignment centers could be housed. Under the heat of public outcry, these "rubber rooms" were finally shut down in the fall of 2010.

Public schools can't improve because teachers are smothered by bureaucracy. To address this system failure, structural reforms such as school-based decision making or parental choice of schools are imperative. Even though funding for public schools has increased over the years, the problem is the lack of standards in running schools. Policy-makers haven't put adequate policies in place to weed out incompetent teachers and ensure students adhere to behavior standards that ensure academic order in classrooms and on school grounds. Additionally, schools need to be more strategic on how data is used to move instruction, the design of instruction, and how interventions are built to support students. Public education reforms fail because they are compromised or sabotaged by the education lobbies, and lack of training for school leaders and teachers.

Tenure is not the only barrier to successful school organization. States decide positions and salary levels without any relationship to a particular school's situation. To foster successful reorganization of schools and more effective and efficient use of teachers, school systems or even individual schools must be able to employ their teaching staff as they see fit and pay them accordingly.

Incentives for teacher excellence based on student performance should be developed and implemented. When teachers are paid and rewarded based on years of service and education only with no incentive built in for student academic success, it is easy for teachers to do the minimum, knowing that they will receive the same pay as the teachers in adjoining classrooms who simply babysit students all day. It is also important to create better lines of communication between administrators, educators, and teachers. Stakeholders need input into decisions about such topics as the makeup of the history curriculum or the daily school schedule.

Educational systems often shift poor teachers from school to school, allowing them to keep their jobs. This practice systemically adds to failure after failure by perpetrating incompetency on a wider group of students. If one incompetent teacher teaches 100 kids a day per year (5 classes of 20 kids) for 30 years, they will negatively impact over 3,000 lives! That portends a colossal negative effect on the lives and chances of success of kids and society as a whole. Keeping one poor teacher in the system makes us lose thousands of opportunities to change lives. We need to change the system to put students first. I am not recommending making lighthearted decisions that affect the livelihood of marginal teachers, but I am saying that protecting and keeping poor teachers is hurting students and school systems. If we can't improve their performance with training, we need to get rid of them.

Teaching is a hard job, and it's not for everyone who thinks they want to be a teacher. Teaching is much more than instruction; it is relationship building, classroom management, instructional creation and delivery, data analysis to improve instruction, and even the willingness to be a pseudo-parent when necessary. These roles and duties carry a lot of responsibility, necessary education, and professional development. It may seem as if I am hard on teachers, but the truth is that teachers are the heartbeat of the school. If the teachers are well taken care of and provided the proper structures by leadership for safety, discipline, trust, collaborative decision-making, strong instructional methodology, data-driven instructional decision making, support, and professionalism, the environment for teachers to thrive will be optimal. I liken this to systems of the body. The heart has to be functioning well for all other parts of the body to work. If the administration is the brain, the teachers are the heart, and the support staffs are the other organs that the body needs to function correctly. If one or two organs fail, it could cause dire consequence for the body, but in most cases the body can still function. The body can even function if there is brain damage, but if the heart stops working, no blood can get to the other organs, and all will shut down. Teachers need to be protected and treated like they are the most vital organ in the body. If the heart is defective, all efforts must be made to revitalize it. In educational terms, teachers must be coached, given time to develop, and treated with respect as professionals. Once coaching, grooming, and developing efforts have been exercised, but no improvements to the heart are made, then it is time for a transplant. Remove the old and replace it with a heart that will function better within the system. The system will be grateful because the poorly functioning heart was putting stress on the other organs. It is easier said than done because often poor teachers are good people who truly aren't meant to teach or at least in the environments they are teaching in. It takes a special person to teach in an urban environment when there are so many factors beyond delivering instruction.

Ultimately, keeping a heart that is only working at 20% capacity is hindering and not helping. In terms of the body, a surgeon would not remove a heart that is working at 20% capacity and then implant it into another patient. That would be killing another system. Districts have to do better, and unions who are unions because they want to protect the rights of educators need to do the humane thing and remove hearts that function below capacity to protect the other hearts within the system. I recommend starting a program that counsels teachers out of teaching when necessary (after documentation, coaching, development, etc.) and provides links to other careers. The district could partner with and create liaison relationships with local businesses to help teachers transition to other careers.

3
SECTION

HOW DO WE CHANGE OUR COMMUNITIES?

BUILDING FAMILY STRUCTURES AND VALUES TO TACKLE ROT

We need solutions to failure among students of color.

In the previous chapters, we discussed the effect and symptoms of the Willie Lynch's curse and how the family structures in black communities are dismally broken. Children are growing up in without father figures and male role models who could have a positive influence. Kids are not learning society's values and good morals. Parents, especially fathers, are supposed to be conduits to pass down morals and important values to their kids and in general, the younger generation. In order for conditions to improve, things have to be done differently; the social norms that put us at a disadvantage have to be broken. Better cultural values must be imbibed, neglect of male children must stop, and healthy relationships with the parents and their children must be established.

The onus is on men to step up, start taking responsibilities of fatherhood by being good examples. Black men need to be present and involved with their families and take an interest in their children's' lives. They should inculcate better habits, better decision making, and more productive lifestyles. Blacks must stop feeding into stereotypes, start being independent, take their destinies into their own hands, and work hard towards making their individual lives better. Individual efforts become an extension into the Black community, thus making the world a better place.

I was on Instagram the other day, and one of my former students posted the following quote, "You are not responsible for the programming you picked up in childhood. However, as an adult, you are 100% responsible for fixing it. When you blame others, you give up your power to change." This quote is powerful and describes exactly what our Black men need to do.

Most Black parents in this country would agree that it is important that families teach children values such as honesty, hard work, and respect for others.

African American fathers are often regarded as the most uninvolved group of parents in our nation. In 2008, after Black teenagers in Philadelphia committed a series of assaults and acts of vandalism, Mayor Michael Nutter singled out African American fathers for especially harsh criticism. "Part of the problem in our community, the Black community," he said, "is that we have too many men making too many babies that they don't want to take care of." President Barack Obama (then a presidential candidate) castigated Black fathers for having "abandoned their responsibilities, and acting like boys instead of men." Common stereotypes portray Black fathers as being largely absent from their families. Black fathers should step up and be responsible by living with (or visiting often if they cannot reside) and taking care of their children financially and emotionally.

We have to gain a better understanding of the negative effects of poor relationships because poor social relationships weaken the health of individuals. In recent years, the term "family values" has become a rallying cry against the increase in nontraditional families in this country. Much of the recent public discourse about women who bear children outside of marriage seems to reflect an underlying assumption that appropriate values are something these women simply do not have. An alleged decline in values, often represented in the media by families headed by single mothers, and especially Black single mothers, has been blamed for a myriad of social problems including unemployment, poor health, school dropout rates and an increase in juvenile crime. The breakdown of the traditional family has been blamed for these problems, so it is not surprising that many people conclude that the logical solution to the problem is the reuniting the traditional family, returning our country to the "good old days," when values were presumably different and better. Consistent with such thinking, recent years have seen an increase in governmental programs and policy proposals at both the local and national levels aimed at bolstering the traditional family structure, or otherwise encouraging what are presumed to be family values. Our community can start the change by deciding what values about family structure they wish to pass on to the next generation.

Although traditional formal marriage and the ideal of the nuclear family is promoted in the rhetoric of family values, historically, the extent to which this society has valued formal marriage has not been governed by some consistent standard that has equally supported the nuclear family structure throughout society. In our history, formal public policies and institutionalized racism have acted in tandem to force many Black families to develop alternatives to the traditional nuclear family structure. During slavery, the government condoned and promoted a system in which marriage and family among slaves had no legal status. Slave parents had no recognized authority over their children; slave children were subject to sale by their owners. The idea of what constitutes a family was manipulated, different between races, to serve the slave masters' economic interests. Thus, the legal principle was developed that the status of a slave child followed that of the mother. The institution of slavery had a profound effect on the structure of Black families. Between 1880 and 1915, between twenty-five and thirty percent of urban Black families were headed by females. (Jones J., 1985)

The negative effects of increased rates of pregnancy and single parenthood in the Black community are well known as they place these families at higher risk for certain outcomes. Black adults who are the products of single-parent families are generally less successful than adults who as children grew up in two-parent homes. Moreover, having a low income is one of the greatest disadvantages associated with single parenthood, along with low levels of parental involvement and high levels of residential mobility. The male has historically been considered the head of the family, a status which was, until recently, affirmed in the law through a whole host of legal rules. It is also deeply ingrained in our culture. In addition to the ways in which adults are disadvantaged, lower rates of African American marriage may be especially problematic for African American children. According to a 2004 U.S. Census Bureau report, over 25 million children live apart from their biological fathers, a reality that touches one out of every three (34.5%) children in America.

In addition, nearly two in three (65%) African American children, compared to four in ten (36%) Hispanic children, and nearly three in ten (27%) White children live in fatherless homes. In addition, when compared to children in single-parent families, children raised in married-parents homes have better emotional and physical health and engage in fewer risky behaviors including premarital sex, substance abuse, delinquency, and suicide. Furthermore, children with married parents do better academically and fare better economically than children reared by low-income, single parents. Strong marriages also provide a positive model of intimate relationships because children raised in intact homes are more likely to view marriage positively and maintain long-term marriages.

In part, family values rhetoric represents feelings of frustration about the many problems that exist in this society. It reflects a conclusion that these problems can only be solved through acts of individual will; in other words, if you change the way people think, you will change the way they act, and thereby change society. Research shows that children raised without fathers are disproportionately represented in statistics concerning failure in school, involvement with the criminal justice system and other problems. Strengthening African American families can be an important means to improve the life conditions of African Americans. When African American boys live with their father in the home, particularly their married fathers, they typically receive substantially more parental support. As a result of this parenting, African American boys with married parents are markedly less likely to become delinquent, and they also tend to do better in school. Marriage clearly matters for African Americans. There is strong evidence that solid marriages are vital sources of economic security and greater psychosocial well-being. Generally, married couples are better off financially and save more than divorced, never-married, and widowed households. (R.R.Rindfuss et al., 1990)

My wife and children are with me. My wife has been with me since I was fifteen years old. We have time periods apart, but the majority of our adult lives we have been together. She is a strong woman who believes in family and her husband. After having witnessed so many dysfunctional relationships, I did not know exactly how to treat her. I had an idea because I saw my grandfather treat my grandmother well. My family (my mother in particular) instilled good morals and values in me. My maternal grandparents also played a huge part in my character development. I wouldn't be the person I am today without them.

In conclusion, the family structure in Black communities has to improve to provide a good foundation and environment for the male child to flourish, get an education, change his life, and, in the long run, impact others.

SEPARATING REALITY FROM THE FANTASY OF THE ENTERTAINMENT WORLD

Earlier in this book, we critically analyzed the influence that the entertainment industry has on our children and youths, and the overarching effect it could have on their future decisions, actions, and values, affecting the Black community and society.

The celebrity culture and media have tremendous reach; kids are more influenced by social media, television, and music stars than teachers, doctors, and politicians. The entertainment industry promotes fantasy to the public, and kids are especially susceptible. Adults need to intervene and teach children how to separate reality from the fantasy of the entertainment world. I encourage families to explore media together and discuss their educational value. Children should be encouraged and taught to critically analyze what they see in the media instead of gobbling up everything they see as factual and real. When kids don't know how to draw the line between what is real and what is fantasy, they may engage in deliberate acts and risk-taking behaviors with negative consequences. Watch for warning signs of this confusion. Children and youths can be impulsive.

Brain imaging research shows that teens are more sensitive than adults to the rewards of situations or activities, yet are less sensitive to risks. The National Institutes of Health has shown that the prefrontal cortex, a region of the brain associated with inhibition of risky behavior, doesn't fully develop until age twenty-five. On the plus side, teens are rapid learners because their brains are still developing, but also find it easier to develop dangerous habits.

Parents can control risky behaviors by ensuring kids are supervised. For instance, they can enroll teens in healthy after-school programs where adults are present. Boys should be taught from a young age that their decisions and the choices they make are very important and every action has consequences. They need to be taught to be accountable for their actions and live with the consequences. Parents can reward good behavior instead of emphasizing punishment of negative behavior. Find incentives that get your child motivated; for example, give a bonus in allowance when a child does something good rather than taking away money as a penalty.

Due to the low standard of living and high level of poverty in the Black community, children tend to indulge in escapism. Escapism is the tendency to seek distraction and relief from unpleasant realities, especially by seeking entertainment or engaging in fantasy. The ultimate goal of escapism is the destruction of self. When there is an aspect of life that one wants to escape from, one's fantasies act as a means of dissociating the mind from the "you" that possesses these qualities. With enough repetition, you come to view yourself as a totally separate entity from the one who has these negative traits or circumstances. Although only in rare instances does it get so extreme, partial destruction of the "self" and dissociation are common.

When we practice escapism, we try to avoid "spending time" with ourselves. Rather than engage in healthy introspection or meaningful social interaction, we occupy ourselves endlessly with social media, television, email, video games, gambling, drugs and alcohol, and so on. In fact, individuals watch TV when they don't want to think. Escapism is the opposite of mindfulness and allows us to numb ourselves to realities that we do not want to accept. It allows us to avoid feelings of shame or emotional pain. By imagining ourselves as people who do not have the constraints that we do, or who possesses something that we lack, we can experience that imagined life without having to do the work (and have the luck) necessary to achieve it.

Internet addicts engage in interactive activities online (gaming, participating in forums, etc.) to compensate for their lack of interpersonal interaction in real life. It seems reasonable that there is some psychological cost to living outside of reality. The use of escapist and avoidant coping, including the excessive withdrawal into technology, is a recipe for negative feelings and disconnection from others. To solve this problem, children should be in environments where they can interact with other humans, they should not be isolated. Environments such as book clubs, debate clubs, and children's groups should be encouraged. Moreover, children should spend more time reading, or engaging in indoor and outdoor sports or intellectual activities and spend time away from smartphones, the Internet, video games, television, and other forms of technology that minimize in-person interactions. Nowadays, kids spend so much time with media that they have few chances to explore other things they're good at, activities that could boost their self-esteem.

PARENTS SHOULD WORK ON IMPROVING THE SELF-ESTEEM OF THEIR KIDS.

Having a sense of responsibility gives you personal power because you are not at the mercy of external forces. A new study about youth found that watching television lowers self-esteem in Black children. This happens because while White male TV characters tend to hold positions of power in prestigious occupations, TV roles of girls and women tend to be less positive and more one-dimensional. Female characters are often sexualized, and success is often measured based on physical appearance. Black men and boys are often criminalized on TV, which can affect viewers' feelings of self-worth. Self-esteem has significant behavioral and emotional ramifications, and it is often correlated with motivation, persistence, and academic achievement, especially in children.

Self-esteem is how we feel about ourselves, and our behavior clearly reflects those feelings. Self-esteem is critical to success. For example, a child with high self-esteem will not be easily influenced, and the advantages include that the child will be able to act independently, assume responsibility, and handle negative and positive emotions. Parents must show that they accept their children, care for them, and help them find positive personal identities. Kids need to feel that they are important. Adults can put an incentive system in place in which they reward children for good deeds and behavior from time to time. In addition, parents and guardians should be a good example to the children; they should be available as a resource for guidance and for instilling feelings of positive self-worth. Our children need to recognize that parents are their first and their real role models, not the people they see on television. Children want to know that their parents are there for them. Parents should be advocates and activists for their children. They should be good role models, and can start by building their own self-esteem. In general, the more positive the parents' self-esteem, the more positive the child's self-esteem will be.

Teach your children to practice making positive self-statements. Self-talk is very important in everything we do because words guide behavior choices and emotions. Psychologists have found that negative self-talk is behind depression and anxiety. What we think determines how we feel, and how we feel determines how we behave. Therefore, teach children to be positive about how they talk to themselves. Teach and help them to build positive images and find their identities. They should learn self-discipline. To help children learn self-discipline, parents needs to adopt the roles of coaches and teachers rather than that of disciplinarians and punishers (except when necessary. Yeah, sometimes you just got to kick a little ass).

THE UNITY OF SCHOOLS AND COMMUNITIES

To increase Black male success in higher education, the Black community has to make education a priority and encourage children to go and stay in school. The Black male child must take advantage of education; dropping out of school, disciplinary issues such as drug use, rebellious and criminal behavior should be frowned at. Communities can start setting this priority from individual households by teaching children moral values, ethics, and culture. The Black community can provide tangible support by ingraining in children, youth, and adult that in order to realize their full human potentials, standards have to improve. Failure to place value on education is a perfect recipe for failure. Community members should regard the schools as the hub of their community and the place to go where you can have a safe, healthy, fair, and moral start in life. Hence, male children of color can grow up to be strong men and leaders of their communities in the future.

In addition, schools and communities have to unite and hold each other accountable. The communities should support the school, and there are several ways to do so. Parent Teachers Organizations (PTO) can organize periodic conferences where teachers and parents can deliberate, brainstorm, and make decisions on issues pertaining to educating the male child. Issues to be discussed include challenges the school is facing, children's needs, and how to tackle these issues. If the community and school came together as a united front to solve the debacle of apathy and other bedeviling education issues, the male child's lot in life and education would improve.

The school and community can also work together by organizing mentoring programs for the students. Black men in positions of leadership should meet with students of color at schools, as well as allowing students to visit them in their offices. When young Black men see and have access to successful Black men in a structured form of mentorship, it serves as a positive influence, provides role models, and is a source of inspiration. I might not have made it out of The Projects if I didn't have few role models around me who I aspired to be like and who continuously encouraged me to be whatever I wanted to be. Parents need to actively seek out role models who shatter negative stereotypes of African-American lives. The primary purpose of positive role models willing to be mentors is to provide children with much-needed positive guidance to counteract cultural stereotypes and media influences.

Understanding how successful Black males were able to avoid the pitfalls and hardships that beset others may help the Black community to devise ways to protect and provide support for the young ones. Families, and I am especially speaking to Black mothers, you have to stop making excuses for your young men and work with the community instead of against it. We have to train our Black male children and teens to be strong mentally and physically. I often witness parents protecting their children's negative behaviors and defending their children even when they are wrong. That is NOT protection. It is enabling, teaching, and reaffirming negative, counterproductive behaviors that will continue into adulthood. An old adage in the Black community proclaims that it takes a village to raise a child. Sixty years ago, everyone in a neighborhood looked out for and had a hand in shaping the character and behavior of children in the community. The joke was if the neighbor caught you doing something wrong you would get a *butt whoopin'* by them and then when you got home, your parents would give you another whoopin'. I'm not suggesting that you whip other people's kids, but I am suggesting that as parents we develop a mindset of working together as a community. When members of the community or school witness your child doing wrong, you and they should stand together and unite to create a unified front to retrain and reteach your child appropriate ways to act. I've witnessed parents watch a video of their child breaking a window on video and heard them say it was not their child. Laugh Out Loud at this mentality. Those parents promoted more negative behaviors by not holding their child accountable for their actions. What did they think they were doing by siding with the negative behavior? Ultimately, we have to break the cycle of allowing our children to be mentally weak and force them to be accountable and live the consequences of their behaviors.

Problems in education do not happen in isolation and are the result of faulty judgments, policies, and mindsets. The government and policymakers have to revamp the educational system; the policies involved in running the entire systems of schools should be reviewed. Ineffective policies should be replaced, government subventions should be invested wisely, and quality of training for teachers should be increased. The standards for the teacher competency should be increased, while unproductive, and incompetent teachers should be relieved of their duties and replaced.

The nation's public school system lacks adequate financial resources; therefore, more funds should be allocated to the system. In addition, policymakers should involve members of the community, specifically parents and guardians, in decisions and policies that affect Black students. In order to encourage strong community input, policymakers should maintain close ties with the communities through a community-based advisory board. The board should consist of a wide range of stakeholders proportionate to the community's demographics.

Disciplinary practices should be reviewed so that schools should be more nurturing and supportive. We want students to see schools as a source of opportunity for a good life rather than an inhospitable place that should be avoided. Changing the culture and structure of schools so that African American male students come to regard them as sources of support for their aspirations and identities will be a positive step towards making high levels of academic achievement the norm rather than the exception. However, standards of discipline should not be compromised. In the case of disciplinary issues involving Black students, communities and families must be proactive by teaching moral values from a young age and teaching the negative consequences of crime and other actions. Black students must be taught the importance of respecting authority; they should not be rude or disobedient to their teachers and educators so that they won't run into trouble in school. Parents often tell students the right thing to do with regard to behavior towards adults, but then show a strong disdain for authority in their personal lives. Children have a hard time differentiating between which adults and which authorities they should respect and which do not warrant or require respect. Mistrust of the legal system often creates this type of confused thinking. Parents need to be proactive and not send mixed messages because they confuse children and lead to children's attitudes of disrespect toward teachers and authority figures.

The role the Black community can play in improving Black male education includes teaming up to set up foundations to encourage education of Black youths. A foundation can organize fundraising and award scholarships to brilliant students. Furthermore, community plays a significant role in education when families create environments that enable children to have peace of mind and calm. Kids who are unsettled because of turmoil or challenges at home can't focus and perform optimally in school. Proactive communities encourage stable homes where parents are there for the kids, monitor and manage behavior, and provide for and protect them. Father's presence can contribute to the economic and social wellbeing of a child.

Families in the community should support the efforts made in schools by monitoring the students at times when kids are not at school. Students should spend valuable time studying, practicing, and working on assignments.

Unity and teamwork between school and parents are exemplified at Green Tech High Charter School where parents are kept informed of students' efforts through conferences, monthly progress reports, report cards, phone calls, and notes. Parents may be asked to help teach their child specific skills such as getting organized, remembering homework, learning to be responsible, and managing anger in a mature way. If parents are asked to assist staff with their child's educational development, specific information is provided on ways to help the student. If there is a severe or recurring problem, parents are asked to help staff teach the student an alternative set of behaviors. In addition, every teacher at the school is prepared to work with parents and respond to parental concerns appropriately and expeditiously.

To improve student academic performance, school curriculum should be revamped. Black boys often attend schools where the curriculum emphasizes low-level thinking skills and class work consists of filling out dittoed worksheets, an approach that leaves students minds to wander and leads to disinterest. Black boys require a curriculum that connects to their lives and their interests. Educators need to make school "cool" while they channel boys' abundant energies into productive pursuits.

The quality of teaching is crucial to students' academic success, and Black boys are more likely than other students to have teachers who are unqualified to teach them. Middle school teachers seldom learn how to teach reading and writing effectively to Black boys, because most instructors of teacher education programs don't know how to do it themselves. In addition, there is an unequal representation of African-American men in tenured positions. Symptomatic of the problem is the dearth of minority teachers. For instance in New York City high schools, Black male public school teachers are at times only 2% of the population of teachers! Policymakers should address this disparity by encouraging and training more Black teachers to teach in public schools.

To improve the education of Black males, communities can organize summer community-based programs - with themes of morality and ethics - and after-school male study groups, in which students with specific interests discuss those interests. For example, we could provide education about Black historical figures such as Martin Luther King, Jr., but not just Dr. King. We can also include people who have had a similar impact on society regardless of their area or level of influence.

Another example of unity and teamwork between community and school is found in Bremerton, Washington:

Bremerton School District is proud of its Early Learning Programs. In 2001, Bremerton launched a community-wide plan to increase Kindergarten readiness and made it a district priority to have all children reading at grade level by the end of third grade. Under this new initiative called the Early Childhood Care and Education Group, the District joined forces with area Head Start Programs, preschools, and child care providers. The District is now able to offer access to an Early Childhood TOSA (Teacher on Special Assignment); reading curriculum; math materials; staff development opportunities, and student data from our partners.

Working together, this partnership has resulted in marked gains in student achievement and has provided children with a better quality education. In 2001, only 4 percent of Bremerton Kindergarten students started school knowing their letters. Today, with help from our community partners, that number is now approximately 52 percent! (www.bremertonschools.org)

The community and school teamed up to find solutions to problems confronting education. Their goals were to increase the number of children entering kindergarten with early reading and math skills and to decrease learning difficulties for the students. With buy-in from the community, participating schools share a common language, common goals, and resources. Teachers engage in monthly professional development meetings and remain part of an assessment loop. The school district can now boast of having one of the highest preschool enrollment rates in the country. Educators in Bremerton combined resources and focused dollars on what was needed to help children succeed.

In conclusion, schools alone cannot solve the problem of education of Black males and urban children as a whole, they need to enlist the help of the Black community and work with them. By working together, parents and school staff can help students acquire the skills that will increase opportunities for success throughout life.

CHANGING OUR MINDSETS

To keep male students of color from failing and to improve their life outcomes, mindsets need to change, and people need to be willing and ready to do life differently. We have to break free from Willie Lynch's syndrome; the broken mentality has to be repaired, the broken family structure has to be mended.

In the words of legendary singer Bob Marley, "It is time we emancipate ourselves from mental slavery, no one but ourselves can free our minds." (Redemption Song, circa 1979)

Communities need to start acting and doing things differently. Youths and elders have to start making education a priority. Everybody wants to be successful, has dreams of a better life with prosperity, wants to change their situations, but success cannot be achieved by mere wishes. The saying "if only wishes were horses, beggars would ride" (16th century English Proverb) rings true here. Black males need to realize that wealth, as publicized in the media and flaunted in the music videos, can be attained legally without getting involved in crime and risking involvement in the criminal justice system, conviction, and incarceration. Black males have to be decisive, choose right paths to better lives, start looking up to good roles models, and stay away from bad friends, gangs, and negative influences. We have to realize (and teach our sons) that our destinies are in our hands, and we alone have the power to decide the outcome.

It is important and normal as a youth to have great dreams, but there is a thin line between dreams and fantasy. Youth should not just indulge in escapism where they separate reality from fantasy, as it can result in psychological harm. Instead, they should aspire to become great and at the same time take urgent and measured steps towards the attainment of their goals. Simple steps and actions, such as taking more time to study and reading motivational and self-development books and autobiographies of contemporary leaders and successful people can help youth find their identities. These actions can change habits, attitudes, and lifestyles. Determination and perseverance are paramount to achieving personal dreams and goals because nothing good comes easily, and there are numerous challenges and pitfalls on the road to success. Teach children personal evaluation, and evaluate yourself from time to time to see if you are where you intended to being life. Have you achieved your goals? Why or why not? What can you do to make them happen now? Share your goals, progress, and plan of action with your young people so they can learn how to become successful and plan to achieve their goals.

Black males from The Projects encounter many more obstacles to success than more affluent males. Among these are the environment that they grow up in, the syndrome of broken family structure, single moms, and absent dads resulting in few or no father figures or role models to look up to for positive influence and inspiration. The educational system is not structured to efficiently meet the needs of Black students. These situations are exacerbated by apathy and inactivity of the older generation and their failure to take responsibility and emancipate themselves from mental slavery and the Willie Lynch curse. To stop the cycle from perpetuating to future generations, we have to take urgent steps of change.

As a community, we have the power to get involved. With unity of voice and action, we can make things happen, keep Black boys from failing, and improve their chances of success in life. Starting with each individual, we need to take a stand and contribute to the solution to educating Black males effectively. If each household, whether parental, guardian, or grandparent showed love and good modeling, we would see immediate improvement. Supportive parenting combined with positive discipline that is not unnecessarily harsh would encourage children to grow strong in morals and actions. We have to change kids' role models. Wouldn't it be great if we could get entertainment stars to act and use their talents in ways that would positively influence the kids that look up to them. African American leaders should also use their leadership positions to positively influence the youth.

Black communities and stakeholders in education should work on the school system and effect improvements. PTO should be taken advantage of, and interaction between school administrators and policymakers should be encouraged for the betterment of education as it affects Black males and all children of color. As members of the community, after reading this book, decide to meet a Black male child and plant the seed of hope in him. Afterward, you must stay with that young man and cultivate the relationship. Your efforts will cause growth beyond belief and create opportunities for that young person to become a future distinguished leader.

Dare to step out and make an extra effort with a concentrated focus on planting a seed and cultivating it as well.

4

SECTION

EDUCATION IS THE NEW FORM OF CIVIL RIGHTS

XI

THE LEARNED HELPLESSNESS THEORY

Picture this scenario for a moment:

The bell rings and students begin pouring into the classroom, slowly putting away their backpacks and trickling to their desks to prepare for the day's lesson. Now that they are all seated, you hand out math worksheets to get them ready for a little mental warm up. Suddenly, a sea of whining fills the classroom. "I can't do this," and "These are all hard problems," and "I give up," and "How do you do these? I don't know how!"

Familiar with this scenario? It is all too common.

Why are so many children failing in school? What turns students off to school and aborts learning in children of varying ability levels? What makes students listless and inattentive and sometimes disruptive? What makes them choose not to complete work? What makes them give up quickly when faced with tasks that are difficult? What makes them self-conscious and anxious when they must read aloud or take a test?

As educators and parents, we most often see children with anxieties about task performance and ability to succeed as passive and afraid to try. Exerting effort to them may seem so futile that they give up trying. These students develop self-defeating strategies that eventually lead to the very failures that they are attempting to avoid. They strive for unattainable goals while procrastinating and only accomplishing work that requires minimal effort. They may become depressed or exhibit anger. They may feel that they are "too stupid" to learn and stop trying. Even before students know the assignment, they feel defeated. This is known as *learned helplessness*, a psychological condition in which a student "has learned to act or behave helpless in a particular situation, even when they have the power to change their unpleasant or even harmful circumstance" (Seligman, 1975).

Psychologist Martin Seligman carried out an experiment. He placed three dogs in different groups. Group 1 was given electric shock which they could easily turn off. Group 2 received shocks regardless of what they did. Group 3 was the control group and was not exposed to any shocks. Later all three groups were put in boxes and received shocks. The boxes were low enough for them to help themselves and jump out. Group 1 who had been able to stop the shocks, and Group 3 with no shocks received shocks reacted the same way; they jumped out of the box. Guess what Group 2 did? They were the dogs that received shocks in the first part of the experiment and had no control to stop them. These dogs made no effort to escape; they simply laid down and whimpered. They had learned to be helpless. Seligman tried a similar experiment with noise and humans and had similar results. In both the dog and the human experiments, having no control over their circumstances and no way to stop the unpleasant stimuli caused participants to relinquish control and resign themselves to helplessness, a learned behavior.

Seligman believed that the learned helplessness "phenomenon is comprised of three different parts (a) an undermining of one's motivation to respond; (b) a retardation of one's ability to learn that responding works; and (c) an emotional disturbance, usually depression or anxiety" (1975).

Typically, students who are depressed about past failures "begin to doubt their intellectual abilities, and this leads them to doubt that they can do anything to help overcome their difficulties. They then lessen their achievement efforts, particularly when faced with difficult material, and this leads in turn to continued failure" (Sutherland and Singh, 2004). Obviously, students who are wrapped up in learned helplessness get the overwhelming feeling that they will never get problems correct. Unlearning learned helplessness is a difficult task.

Lack of interest in education is a learned behavior that oppresses minorities of all demographics across this great nation. My school, an all-boys charter school composed of over 95% African American males of which 80% live in poverty, just reached milestones of 90%+ graduation rate, 100% acceptance to college, and millions of dollars in scholarship money. I ask myself how this happen when a good percentage of our young men come in with an attitude that doesn't value education, an attitude that I have seen too frequently among young men and women of color. So how do you change a value and bad habit? You change it by retraining habits, and establishing new rituals and routines to replace the old ones.

Forty years ago a young person could choose not go to college, work at factory job such as Kodak, and immediately become a middle-class citizen. That is no longer the case. Unfortunately, civil rights, or rather, the level of rights, has always been attached to social class and income. The more you make, the more rights you have. Apart from entrepreneurship, how can someone equalize the playing field in a market that respects education as a sole measure of value and worth? Get an education!

Young people in our society often value the wrong things. I praise young people who are on the right path, but now turn corners to take a serious look at those who are not. Some questions come to mind that beg answers: Why isn't education valued the way it used to be? Does technology create a sense of immediate gratification that is given instead of earned? How do we get our society to value education again? Where was respect for education lost?

The Civil Rights Act of 1964 which banned racial segregation and discrimination is iconic of the years of civil struggle and fighting that occurred so that Black children could have educational opportunities equal to Whites. The outcomes of the Civil Rights Movement seem to have lost their potency and value for the current generation of students. Education is the new Civil Rights Movement. With a positive mindset of appreciation for those who came before us and struggled for our freedom, we can take advantage of educational opportunities and unlock the world and the rights thereof as we experience equality and freedom of choice denied to those who do not pursue education. Education is our true freedom, something that can't be taken away.

How do you take advantage of educational opportunities? You do something every day. Do you brush your teeth? Yes, I want to believe you do. You are looking confused right now, and thinking, "Huh? Did he really ask that?" Let me explain. Most people brush their teeth a few times daily. It is a routine. Having good hygiene is taught, and practiced by having a daily routine that becomes a value and good habit. Tony Schwartz said, "Incremental change is better than ambitious failure; success feeds on itself." Practice builds routines, routines build habits, and habits build the fabric of lives. The habit of education opens doors and creates scholars who want to be free, who want a higher level education that gives them freedom of choice.

5
SECTION

RITUALS AND ROUTINES FOR RUNNING EFFECTIVE SCHOOLS SO CHILDREN DON'T FAIL

STRATEGIES FOR RUNNING EFFECTIVE SCHOOLS

Best instructional practices are specific and deliberate teaching methods aimed at fostering positive interaction in the classroom. They are products of years of research to learn what works for effective student learning.

In 2013, educational researcher John Hattie unveiled his findings in his book, *Visible Learning for Teachers: Maximizing Impact on Learning*. His research goals included helping teachers see and understand learning through students' eyes. Hattie spent more than fifteen years researching influences on achievement of K-12 children. His findings linked student outcomes to several highly effective classroom practices. Highlighted here are a few of those practices:

1. Teaching for Understanding and Teacher Clarity

Challenge students to think and use their own knowledge to solve problems and connect ideas. Clarify the purpose of educational activities and learning goals, and provide explicit criteria for successful completion of learning objectives. Ideally, teachers would incorporate models and examples of good finished work to engage visual learners, and set the standard of acceptable performance by letting students see what the finished product looks like.

• Planning before each lesson

Learning objectives remain constant across students, but teachers must take diversity into consideration when planning lessons. What works for one student in a class may not work for another, necessitating teacher planning that approaches learning with *Differentiated Instruction* to reach all students.

Teachers who use Differentiated Instruction know their students well enough through pre-assessment of student knowledge, skills, and understanding to decide what instructional techniques will result in student success across the curriculum and student demographics. Lesson Plans based on Differentiated Instruction often provide opportunities to build relationships between the teacher and student and among fellow students through ongoing assessment and interaction. With the advent of technology, digital sources can be used to leverage efforts to differentiate instruction because the digital sources can easily be edited or adjusted to address student learning needs. Because of its flexibility, a variety of formats engages learners with different strengths to explore topic under investigation. The relationship of the primary source to the topic under study may be either concrete or abstract. Primary sources may require high levels of background knowledge and vocabulary or may have needed vocabulary printed right on the source. This variation in sources helps teachers add rigor to the curriculum for all students while meeting students at their individual academic level.

• Classroom Discussion

Teachers need to frequently step offstage and facilitate classroom discussions that include all students. Doing so allows students to learn from each other. It's also a great opportunity for teachers to do formative assessment (through observation) to determine how well students are grasping new content and concepts.

• Literacy Instruction

Literacy instruction teaches specific strategies to enable students to locate, comprehend, evaluate, and apply knowledge by reading the materials created by real life and includes content-related vocabulary instruction. Primary sources are compelling reading materials for all content areas in the curriculum. The mysterious context, historical vocabulary, and different formats challenge students to read, think, and use what they know about a subject to make sense of the primary source.

• Feedback

Learners won't know they are moving forward without a consistent feedback mechanism that informs them of their growth. *You cannot grow what you don't measure.* Along with individual feedback (written or verbal), teachers need to provide whole-group feedback on patterns they see in the collective class growth and in areas requiring additional study and practice. Students also need to be given opportunities to provide feedback *to the teacher* so that she can adjust the learning process, materials, and instruction to better meet student needs and hold student attention.

• Formative Assessments

In order to provide students with effective and accurate feedback, teachers need to assess frequently and routinely to determine where students are in relation to the learning goals or end products of the unit being studied (summative assessment). Hattie recommends that teachers spend the same amount of time on formative evaluation during the learning process as they do on summative assessment.

- **Metacognitive Strategies**

Students are given opportunities to plan and organize, monitor their own work, direct their own learning, and to self-reflect along the way. When we provide students with time and space to be aware of their own knowledge and their own thinking, student ownership increases. Also, it gives students the opportunity to be independent and immersed in their learning activity. Students who engage in metacognitive learning strategies can be taught, and students who are proficient in using them build academic confidence and commitment.

- **Technology Integration**

Technology Integration provides students with real-world use of technology in the classroom as part of unique lesson plans designed to simultaneously teach content and provide practice using technology. The 21st century is technology-driven, and young people leverage it heavily, particularly mobile technology that push the frontiers of social interaction.

Teachers can effectively use technology to teach literacy skills, thinking routines, and content knowledge while developing technology expertise. Students are motivated to solve problems through online research to build and increase understanding of the curriculum.

- **Collaborating with Colleagues**

Great teachers are earnest learners. As iron sharpens iron, so one person sharpens another (Proverbs 27:17, NIV) Teachers need time to converse with colleagues and talk about what research-based, best classroom practices look like in the context of their unique learning environment, paying attention to what their students need to know, already know, etc.

Putting Hattie's instructional practices into effective use can cause our kids turn around and head in a positive direction so that no child experiences failure.

2. Positive and Working Teacher-Student Relationships

The effects of positive and working teacher-student relationships in our schools draw students into the learning process and promotes their desire to learn (on the assumption that the content material of the class is engaging, age-appropriate, and well matched to the student's skills). A student who feels a strong personal connection to her teacher, talks with her teacher frequently, and receives more constructive guidance and praise rather than criticism is more likely to trust her teacher, show more engagement in learning, behave better in class, and achieve at higher academic levels than she might have if she didn't have the positive connection to the teacher. Improving students' relationships with teachers has important, positive, and long-lasting implications for both students' academic and social development.

Improving students' relationships with their teachers will not produce gains in achievement solely as a result of the relationship. However, those students who have close, positive, and supportive relationships with their teachers will attain higher levels of achievement than those students with more conflict in their relationships. Teachers who have positive relationships with their students make classroom environments more conducive to learning and meet students' developmental, emotional, and academic needs.

Now that the effect of a positive relationship between a teacher and her student has been established, how can a teacher create this kind of working relationship?

- **Know your students, their interests, and their temperaments**

Knowing students' interests can help the teacher create examples to match those interests. The teacher needs to understand that in many schools, especially in big cities like Los Angeles, children come from different cultures and backgrounds. A teacher needs to understand the value of students' senses of belonging, which can be of great value in building self-worth for minority students. If the teacher demonstrates an understanding of a student's culture and interests, it creates a bond and closer relationship between student and teacher. For example, if a student who loves basketball comes to you for help with a math problem, it might be easier for you to use examples in basketball to provide him with a response that he'll quickly understand.

If a student who speaks Spanish or French at home comes to you with a question about English vocabulary, you might answer his question and then ask him what the word is in his native language, and how he'd use it in a sentence. This type of specific responding shows that you care about your students as people and that you are aware of their unique strengths (i.e., fluency in another language).

Knowing a student's temperament can help you construct appropriate learning opportunities and environments. For example, if a girl in your class is particularly distractible, you can support her efforts to concentrate by offering her a quieter area in which to work without distraction so that she can thrive and become better academically. If a boy in your classroom is very shy, appears engaged but never raises his hand to ask questions, you can assess his level of understanding of a concept in a one-on-one conversation at the end of class.

• Give students useful feedback

Be intentional about *how* you give feedback to your students. Your mannerisms and body language speak volumes. Students pay more attention to your nonverbal cues than to your words. If possible, record yourself while teaching to see exactly what kind of feedback you are giving. In Stanford Univeristy Psychologist Carol Dweck's book, *Mindset: The New Psychology of Success* (2007), she proposing praising students' efforts instead of their intelligence. Here are a few questions that you can ask yourself to guide your feedback process:

1. Are you giving students meaningful feedback that shows you care about them and growing their knowledge and skills, or are you constantly telling your students to hurry?

2. In your conversations, are you focusing on what your students have accomplished, or are you concentrating your comments on what they have not yet mastered?

3. Do your body language, facial expressions, and tone of voice show your students that you are interested in them as people with feelings, aspirations, and dreams?

4. Are you telling students to do one thing, yet exhibiting different behaviors? For example, do you tell your students to listen to each other, but then look bored when one of them talks to the class? Be sure that the feedback you give to your students conveys the message that you are supporting their learning and that you care about them.

5. Are you paying more attention to some students than to others?

Answering questions like these will go a long way to help you identify where you need to intensify efforts to help students succeed academically right now because no student must fail this year, at least not on your watch!

• Create a positive and fun learning environment

One of the best ways to make students listen in class and foster good relationships with them is to make the environment fun while linking concepts and skills to their own experiences.

Build fun into the things you do in your classroom. Plan activities that create a sense of community so that your students have opportunities to see the connections between what they already know and the new things they are learning, as well as have the time to enjoy being with you and the other students. Set high learning expectations, but make sure you provide social and emotional support.

• Encourage respect

Teachers who demonstrate respect towards their students automatically win favor because respect encourages students to be active learners. Not only should you treat students with respect, but you must also insist that students treat each other with respect. I always tell teachers that it is important to be respected first, and liked second. If your students respect you, they will not disrespect you, but if they like you, they will work harder for you. The issue of respect extends to name-calling and bullying as well, and neither should be tolerated in your classroom.

Children who are teased or bullied by other children are victimized by their peers and find learning difficult. They are not only stressed out by trying to achieve academically, but also dealing with the emotional pain and confusion caused by the names they are given by their classmates. Disrespect to fellow students is destructive, demeaning, and destroys self-esteem. Don't allow it in your classroom!

• Correct students in constructive ways

Correcting and disciplining students eliminate inappropriate and unwholesome behaviors is both an art and science, and it doesn't have to be a negative part of your job. In fact, you can build positive relationships when you correct students.

After several years of teaching, most teachers have students return to visit them. Often those visitors are the students who were difficult and challenging, but one you spent the most time helping, correcting, and guiding. They remember because you made a difference and built positive relationships with them. You might have been the only person in their lives at the time who was a positive influence, and they will continue to come back and remember you for years to come.

The aim of correcting students should be to have them reflect on what they did, be sorry that they disappointed you and themselves, and learn to make a better choice in the future. It should not be that they go away thinking, "I hate my teacher. I'm going to be sure I don't get caught next time." The difference in students' reactions to being disciplined is often related to the manner in which you correct them. If you allow students to keep their dignity even as you correct them sternly, then you increase the chances that they will reflect on their behavior and make wiser choices in the future. The correction process is counterproductive if you communicate bitterness, sarcasm, low expectations, or disgust. The goal is to provide a quick, fair, and meaningful consequence while simultaneously communicating that you care for and respect the student.

- ## Actionable advice to follow when correcting students

Imagine that an incident happened which saw Tim slap Jane because Jane made an unsavory remark about his dad. The following will help you in taking the necessary and effective disciplinary actions:

Do a review what happened.

Sit Tim down and discuss the incident with him. Begin with fact finding to be sure that you are appropriately correcting the student. The worst way to step into the incident is to unfairly discipline a student or to discipline the wrong student.

Identify and accept the student's feelings.

Explain to Tim that you understand why it upset him to hear somebody call his dad a name and that you, too, would be upset if someone made a snide remark about your dad. This step communicates that you respect and understand his feelings but do not accept his actions.

Review alternative actions.

Brainstorm with Tim some alternate choices he could have made, such as ignoring the remark or reporting it to a teacher.

Explain the school's policy as it applies to the situation.

Reiterate the school policy on fighting, and the consequences of hitting other students, which might include suspension from school.

Let the student know that all students are treated equally.

Make sure that Tim understands that all students must adhere to the school's policies and that any student who breaks the rules is subject to predetermined consequences.

Activate an immediate and meaningful consequence.

Communicate with the office about what happened and send Tim to the office.

Let the student know you are disappointed that you have to invoke a consequence to his or her action.

Tell Tim that you are disappointed that his actions require formally involving the office.

Communicate an expectation that the student will do better in the future.

Let Tim know that, although you do not approve of his actions and do not like to send him or any student to the office for disciplinary action, you like him and know that he will make a better choice next time. Also, tell him that you are there to support him and work through this and other issues with him in the future, but appropriate disciplinary actions will have to be taken because it is the right thing to do.

In addition to following these steps when correcting a student, keep in mind some key psychological considerations. First of all, remember to correct the student in a private location. Although it is not always possible to remove a student from the classroom, do your best to prevent visual access by other students as you discipline the erring student. Correcting in public can kick start and amplify feelings of anger, embarrassment, and bitterness; it can also become a sideshow for the other students. Also, when invoking a consequence, you should ask yourself, "How would I want my own children disciplined in a similar situation?" Answering this question will help you treat the student with care and respect. Similar consideration might be to ponder how you would handle the situation if your administrator was watching. Finally, remember to stay calm. The worst thing you can do is invoke disciplinary action when you are angry or upset because your emotional state can influence your objectivity. If necessary, cool off before interacting with the student.

• Steps to Follow After Disciplining a Student

Let's go back to the example of Tim. He earned an office referral because he hit Jane. Here are some actions you could take:

Keep in Touch With the Student.

Follow up with Tim after the disciplinary action, checking to see how he's doing and simply making contact with him so he knows you care about him and still respect him.

Acknowledge Post-Disciplinary Successes.

The next time Tim has difficulty with a student and handles the situation more appropriately (such as by verbalizing his displeasure rather than hitting), acknowledge his positive behavior and praise him for making the right decision.

Don't Give Up Too Quickly.

Finally, don't forget that some students respond negatively to positive attention. In such cases, it may appear that the student doesn't want the positive attention. What may actually be happening is a gradual change in the student's self-concept. When students are used to getting into trouble and having negative attention, it takes a while to break this cycle. Often it is just a matter of time before the student starts to show the positive effects of this attention, so don't give up too quickly!

• Foster Beneficial Classroom Pride

If applied appropriately, pride can be extremely useful in developing positive teacher-student relationships (Kerman et al., 1980). In many classrooms, students are proud that they are behaving and achieving at a high level. In other classrooms, a different type of pride develops when students see themselves as being terrors in the school. This other group prides themselves on being the "baddest" class in the school. The pride that students develop helps shape identities, and these personas drive behaviors. When you recognize student successes, there is less negative pride and an increased likelihood that positive pride will result. As a classroom teacher that is bent on making sure each child succeeds, your goal should be to help students take pride in their accomplishments and positive behaviors instead of their negative behaviors.

• Improving Positive Classroom Pride

Showcasing student work is a great way to demonstrate that you value the work they do and that you take pride in the products of their hands. Displayed work does not have to be perfect or show a significant cross section of the students you have in your class. Just the act of displaying good work done by students with low achievement histories builds self-esteem and pride and encourages them to do better work in the future because you placed value on their efforts. Remember to post work in hallways, the office, and other public areas to increase exposure and student pride. The impact becomes greater when students realize others get to see the great work they are doing. An example of this would be to display all your students' art projects in the hallway and to tell your class,

"You all did a great job on your art projects. I am so proud of all of you that I wanted the whole school to see your exemplary work. That's why I put all your works on display in the hallway."

Publicly asking other staff members to enter the classroom so that they can see a specific accomplishment of your class, such as the way they respond to questions, is a really good way to show off class achievement and stir up student spirits and motivation. However, be careful to speak to the accomplishments of all the students when you use this strategy. If you only speak to the accomplishments of high-achieving students, this tactic will backfire on you.

There are other ways besides academics to help students develop pride. You can publicly recognize acts of kindness, positive citizenship, and athletic accomplishments. You can also let parents know of their child's accomplishments in newsletters, during back-to-school events, and at by allowing parents to review student work at parent-teacher conferences. Recently at my school, we implemented a student showcase. We had each teacher in the building recommend five students to display their work in this showcase. Three out of the five were students who weren't historically high performers. The other two were normally academically astute. We found something good that each one of these students did no matter how small or large and displayed it. I ran a contest for the department with the best display. To acknowledge and show off these students' accomplishments we called in parents, community members, and the school body. This effort built a sense of pride for the scholars and their work, even when three out of the five did not particularly do well in school on a daily basis. Hopefully, the effort motivated low-performing students enough to show them that success was possible with sustained effort.

Brag on your kids every chance you get! Let parents know about high attendance rates, high test scores, and high percentages of homework or assignments completed. In this way, you are enlisting parents to be your partners to improve self-esteem and mold better self-concepts. Consider also that parents don't keep their "good" kids home. They sent you their very best every day. If all parents ever hear from school are negative reports, they dread hearing from school. Parents also may develop a negative mindset over time about their child's capacity for educational accomplishment. By sharing the triumphs in addition to the defeats, you may remold parents' outlooks and cause them to raise their expectations.

Student pride doesn't mean student excellence. Nurture *pride in improvement*. Test scores and daily assignments that go from a *D* to a *C* and homework that starts coming in on time are great opportunities for you to recognize student success and build pride.

When pride is absent, conflict can arise, and teachers must know how to handle it.

3. Understanding the Cycle of Urban Conflict

My first book, *Cyberbullying: Breaking the Cycle of Conflict*, proposed a model for understanding urban conflict. Understanding urban conflict enables educators to better serve youth needs, especially in times of extreme need. When a participant in my study invited another individual to fight, he or she used the phrase, "Now You Gonna Have to See Me." This kind of escalation occurs when a conflict reaches a verbal boiling point, causing the protagonist to feel that something drastic must be done to save face and re-establish respect. Additional steps must be taken to terminate the conflict without the loss of respect and social status, specifically in urban communities.

The participants in my study described how most conflicts that began online and escalated to an invitation to fight, usually unfolded in a public, real-world location, such as at school. The participants purposely followed up on their threats in a public place, such as a crowded school hallway, where both participants loudly presented themselves as unafraid. This strategy was a calculated risk because it could have resulted in a physical altercation. However, the data from my study indicated that the risk was worth taking because the majority of situations ended without physical violence. Often verbal conflict escalated and continued back and forth, with each person trying to embarrass the opposition more than the opposition embarrassed them. Finally, an invitation to fight occurred, followed by a public show of verbal aggression. Most of the time, students got louder in hopes that an adult would intervene. And most of the time, that is what happened.

The desired outcome was that no one fought, and neither lost respect or social status. According to Anderson (1999), respect is viewed as social capital, which is highly valued because other forms of capital may become obsolete and, as such, have no value. The participants in my study divulged that the appearance of a willingness to fight was usually sufficient to squelch peer pressure. Even if they didn't have to actually fight (the ideal outcome), participants needed to avoid the embarrassment of public humiliation at all costs.

Gonick (2004) characterized adolescence as a time when young people feel they can only count on themselves, and when any vulnerability can provoke social anxieties about the world in which they must survive. Winning respect by being willing to fight delivers a message to others that the victor will now be free from persecution and will be granted safe passage in their school and neighborhood (Jones, 2004). The loud commotion in a public place serves to deliver the message. However, the altercation typically gets interrupted by an adult in close proximity, giving the impression that, if unimpeded, the two individuals would have become violent. Once an adult intervened, the burden to resolve the conflict was shifted, and the adolescents were no longer in charge of the outcome. Once the adult facilitated peaceful resolution, the participants indicated that the conflict usually dissipated without the loss of social status or respect. The value of respect in the urban community is pertinent and important to the implications of this research, as illustrated in the "Cycle of Conflict" which was created from my research.

CYCLE OF CONFLICT

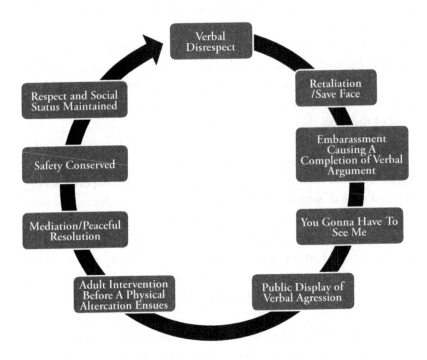

Recommendations for Educator Practice

If you are an urban educator, you already appreciate how critical the concept of respect is to urban youth safety and self-concept. Simply put, kids must maintain respect at all costs, and doing so influences decisions to act aggressively (Bennet-Johnson, 2004). Self-respect should be modeled as an important and necessary component of respect in general. Respect comes from within, not solely from external sources (Richard, Deci, & Edward, 2000). While many of the participants from my study put emphasis on their perceptions of how other people treated them and valued their worth, only two participants discussed the importance of respecting themselves.

Educators can help youth save face by absorbing the conflict and getting involved early before it escalates (Sunburst Visual Media, 2003).

The results from the analysis of my research data showed that mediation between two conflicting parties was effective. An adult mediator should offer mediation as a viable alternative, make it mandatory, be objective, and work towards peaceful outcomes (Tolson, McDonald, & Moriarty, 1990). If students develop an understanding of the educator's policy, it will become an accepted practice and neither party will lose respect because it will appear that the school mandated the resolution.

One technique with the promise of success is to create a contract or written agreement for parties involved to sign when mediation comes to a close. The mediation agreement informs all parties involved of the consequences for breaking agreement (Burell, Zirbel, & Allen, 2003). The consequences must be enforceable. The educator must remain consistent and keep the students accountable if agreements are broken, making a disciplinary example of them, if necessary, to demonstrate to the majority of students just how serious the agreements must be taken. The data from my study revealed that when students mediated, the conflict was often resolved, and students confessed to not wanting to be suspended or arrested for fighting. One potentially unrecognized outcome of working with a skilled mediator is that you learn how to have appropriate face-to-face conversations to resolve conflict, further teaching them that, instead of confronting someone to win respect, they should seek and gain respect by pursuing a mature and peaceful outcome (Tolson et al., 1990).

4. Understand How Students View Themselves

Learned helplessness creates three basic deficits in the child—cognitive, emotional, and motivational—which destroy the child's desire to learn. The motivational deficit impedes learning by aborting the child's desire to respond. Teachers and parents may conclude that the child is not trying, but years of research helps us understand that these children have learned to be helpless to learn. The learned-helpless child believes that he or she has no control over the learning process and after continuous failures, gives up trying because it hurts too much to try—the thoughts of failure overcomes the zeal of trial.

Learned helplessness can be seen as a cognitive deficit in that it is a learned or conditioned response. Mere exposure to uncontrollable situations is not sufficient to make the child helpless, but the expectation of failure in the classroom is sufficient to cause a child to stop trying because of a decrease of logical perception and thinking. The emotional deficit leads to depression, lowered self-esteem, feelings of worthlessness, and suicidal ideation that may be expressed through anger, aggression, running away, stealing, truancy, and other rebellious acts.

A three-part approach is needed and necessary to correct learned helplessness. First, we need to adequately understand the components of learned helplessness to eliminate it. Secondly, we must help children discover the root beliefs and the distorted perceptions they create that cause their self-defeating habits. Thirdly, we must give children the tools they need to change and remediate their distorted beliefs and thereby reduce the deficits.

Martin P. Seligman, the author of *Learned Optimism* (1990), said that "the cure for learned helplessness is not the rediscovery of positive thinking. It does not consist in just learning to say positive things to yourself. Positive statements alone without first clearing out negatives have little if any effect. What is crucial is what you think, changing the destructive things you say to yourself when you fail or have setbacks and making these statements a part of your explanatory style."

Seligman said a person's explanatory style develops in childhood. By third grade, a child already has an optimistic or pessimistic view or style of looking at the world. This style has its roots in the mother's (or predominant parents) explanatory style but is further shaped by criticism from parents, teachers, and other adults. It is also formed from negative life crises such as death, divorce, and unresolved fighting in the family. What goes on in a child's life at home, in the community, and in school has an effect on the child, and there is no neutral reaction. Their experiences (and their perceptions of those experiences) can create a negative explanatory style. Without positive intervention to nip the negative explanation in the bud, the child's future reactions to education and other situations will be negative as the default explanation. Seligman said, "When a child is doing poorly at school, it is all too easy for his teachers, parents, and others to conclude falsely that he is untalented or even stupid. The child may be depressed and learned helpless, and this learned behavior may be preventing him from fulfilling his potential."

Seligman proposed three crucial dimensions of the explanatory style: permanence, pervasiveness, and personalization. It is the permanency of the causes to which individuals attribute bad events that shape their expectations for future events and thereby determine the duration of their depressive episodes and deficits. Students who give up easily believe the causes of failures that happen to them are permanent. They feel that the failures will persist and will always be there to affect their achievement. This permanent expectation of failure creates their learned helplessness symptoms and thus the deficits. Students who resist helplessness believe the causes of bad events are temporary. Compare these two statements: "I failed because I'm not smart," and "I failed because I didn't study hard enough." Permanence is about time. Pervasiveness is about space. Pessimists make global or pervasive explanations for their failures and give up on everything when a failure strikes in just one arena. People who make specific explanations may become helpless in that one part of their lives, but they are okay with other areas. Contrast the statements, "I'm not smart when it comes to school stuff!" to "I don't do well in physics, but I do all right in the other subjects."

Personalization means attaching a failure to characterological causes such as "I am stupid." This personalization causes low self-esteem and depression. A learned helpless explanatory style is characterized by explaining bad events with causes that are permanent in time, global or pervasive in effect, and internal or personal. Whether or not children learn in school depends on the explanatory style they choose. Students who believe that reading failure is based on their lack of ability to be successful (a permanent condition) are convinced that they will have similar reading failure in the future and, therefore, are unlikely to make an effort to change that expectation. If students see their reading failures as due to lack of effort (a temporary and changeable condition), then they may see the possibility of changing.

• Give Positive Reinforcement

Students with a poor track record of success can benefit from positive reinforcement when they do well. You might have to watch close to catch them doing well, but when they do, give positive verbal feedback, tokens, stickers or other rewards for a job well done; anything that will give students a pat on the back and make them feel worthy. Your efforts over time will help build confidence and break down those depressive behaviors that result from learned helplessness. Remember that time is a factor in this remediation process. Giving consistent praise and attention over time for effort and accomplishment will cause the student to make mental connections between performance, praise, and success. Your ongoing efforts to recognize student achievement will go a long way in bolstering confidence and self-esteem and removing the negative explanatory style.

In addition to the positive reinforcement we give students, we also need to be careful of the type of critical responses we give. Criticisms directed towards students like, "I'm very disappointed in you" are often received as personal attacks that further reinforce the underlying depressive emotions of learned helplessness. A student falsely assumes that you are actually saying, "You're no good, you're dumb, you're a failure." Instead, rephrase comments that might be perceived as critical to neutral so they are neutral or positive statements such as, "Maybe you can think of another way to do it." Rephrasing to positive statements leads to healthier academic attitudes. The same outcomes are reflected in the *person versus process* praise dynamic as well. Person praise such as, "I'm very proud of you" leads to student-centered outcomes such as,

"I'm a success, I'm smart. " Process praise such as, "You must have tried really hard!" leads to challenge-centered outcomes like, "I can do this" (Sutherland and Singh, 2004).

As teachers, we have to be conscious of making our criticisms and praise about the process of the problem, not the person, so that the failure can be attributed to the actual work and not to intellectual competence or capacity. Positive reinforcement is helpful over time, so we need to make process praise part of our everyday curriculum.

• Calling on All Students Equitably

When you call on students, be sure to call on all students, not just a few who know the answers or raise their hands frequently. If you only call on a select few, other students will not expect to be called on and may tune you out. When you don't recognize and allow all students to contribute, you are subtly communicating that you have lesser confidence in some students' abilities. Individual students may just "zone out" and believe that you don't expect them to be able to answer your questions, and this disappointing message is further compounded when these students see others being called on to answer questions regularly.

Now, put yourself in their shoes and ponder on this for a moment: What would it communicate to you if your boss always asked other teachers to participate in committee work or special projects, but did not ask you? Conversely, how would you feel if your boss consistently came to you for help on curriculum projects or input on difficult students? Just as you would feel slighted or delighted, students feel the same ways. They develop feelings of self-confidence in their abilities when their teachers go to them for the right answer. Lest you forget, students are humans, too! Just younger and perhaps of lesser-developed emotional intelligence. Calling on all the students in your class—rather than a select few—will help keep students on task and decrease the number of behavior-related problems. Form the habit of asking the question before calling on a student so all students remain engaged because they don't know who you will call on to answer. Keep a tally of which students you call on and how often you call on them so that can make sure you are spreading your attention around to all students. It is tempting to call on your best-performing students, but doing so isolates and alienates students who are not as involved. Call on students who are typically off task or who are low achievers, and allow them to respond, even if it takes a little longer for them to formulate answers.

My teachers use *Total Participation Techniques* to increase student opportunities to be heard and engage in lessons. One example is using individual whiteboards. All students get one and answer every question asked, then display their answers for the class and teacher to see. This practice gives each student a voice and allows the teacher to see what each child is thinking. Teachers use student answers, ideas, thoughts and interests to build rigor and critical thinking skills. In a short time span, this technique improves student performance and increases time on task!

• Increasing Latency Periods When Asking Questions

Increasing latency period (Kerman et al., 1980) is another useful method you can use to communicate that you expect positive results from a student. Latency is the amount of time that elapses between the moment you give a student a response opportunity and the moment you terminate the response opportunity. Kerman and colleagues explain that the amount of time we give students to answer questions is directly related to the level of expectation we have for them. Simply put this is called *Wait Time*. I have seen teachers ask questions and then answer their own questions instead of providing students enough time to think and answer critically. We allot more time to students when we have confidence in their abilities to answer questions. In the same vein, we give less opportunity to students if we have little confidence that they can answer correctly. When you quickly give up on a student who is struggling with a response, what you are making clear to every other student in the classroom is that you don't expect that student to come up with the right answer. In addition, when you give up on a student who initially struggles with a response, the student realizes that all he or she needs to do to "get out of the hot seat" is respond to your question with a confused expression or a poker face.

When you make a conscious effort to give students more time to answer, low-achieving students pay more attention, become more actively involved in discussions, and minimize their behavior issues. Ask a fellow teacher to observe your instruction and record the amount of time you are giving students to answer before you move on to another student. You may learn that you favor one student over another without meaning to show preference.

ALIGNING GOALS TO SCHOOL MISSION, VISION, AND VALUES

Job One for teachers is to create and implement a school system that lets kids succeed. Education leaders are responsible for guiding the process, developing and revising a shared vision, creating and implementing a strong mission, and ensuring that every student can succeed when provided with appropriate, effective learning opportunities. The vision, mission, and goals represent what the school community intends for students to achieve, and is influenced by broader social and policy issues, but the bottom line is the same: continuous improvement, high standards, and academic success. The vision, mission, and goals become the touchstone for decisions, strategic planning, and change processes. They are regularly reviewed and adjusted, using district data to steer needed changes.

Leaders engage the school community to jointly reach consensus about vision, mission, and goals. To be effective, the process should incorporate diverse socioeconomic backgrounds and perspectives in the broader school community and create a consensus to which all can commit. While leaders engage others for input, it is without a shred of doubt that the ultimate responsibility to advocate for and act to increase equity and social justice for all lies with the administration team.

ELEMENTS OF A MISSION AND VISION STRATEGY SO THAT NO CHILD FAILS

1. High expectations for all stakeholders

School vision and goals establish high, specific, and measurable targets for all students and educators. School leaders must:

   a. Use a wide range of information and available data about current working practices and outcomes to shape a vision, mission, and goals with high, measurable expectations for all students and educators.

   b. Tailor the vision, mission, and goals to school, district, state, and federal policies (such as content standards and achievement targets).

   c. Factor in diverse perspectives and craft consensus about vision, mission, and goals that are high but still achievable for every student when provided with appropriate, effective learning opportunities.

   d. Advocate for a specific vision of learning in which every student has equitable, appropriate, and effective learning opportunities and can achieve at high levels.

2. Shared Commitments to Implement the Vision, Mission, and Goals

The process of creating and sustaining the vision, mission, and goals that ensure no child fails should be all inclusive, and build common understandings and genuine commitment among all stakeholders.

Leaders must:

a. Establish, conduct, and evaluate processes used to engage staff and community in a shared vision, mission, and goals.

b. Engage different stakeholders, including those with conflicting perspectives, in ways that build shared understanding and commitment to vision, mission, and goals.

c. Develop shared commitments and responsibilities that are equitably distributed among the staff of the school and the host community for making decisions and evaluating actions and their outcomes.

d. Communicate and act from a shared vision, mission, and goals, so teachers and the community understand, support, and act on them consistently.

e. Advocate for and act on commitments in the vision, mission, and goals to provide equitable, appropriate, and effective learning opportunities for every student.

3. Continuous Improvement toward the Vision, Mission, and Goals

School leaders ensure achievement of all students by guiding the development and implementation of a shared vision of learning, strong organizational mission, and high expectations for every student. Such leaders should:

a. Use or develop data systems and other sources of information (e.g., test scores, teacher reports, student work samples) to identify unique strengths and needs of students, gaps between current outcomes and goals, and areas for improvement.

b. Make decisions based on data, research, and best practices to shape plans, programs, and activities, and regularly review their effects.

c. Use data to determine effective change strategies, engaging staff and community stakeholders in planning and carrying out changes in programs and activities.

d. Identify and remove barriers to achieving the vision, mission, and goals.

e. Incorporate the vision and goals into planning (e.g., strategic plan, school improvement plan), change strategies, and instructional programs.

f. Obtain and align resources (such as learning technologies, staff, time, funding, materials, training, and so on) to achieve the vision, mission, and goals.

g. Revise plans, programs, and activities based on systematic evidence and reviews of progress toward the vision, mission, and goals.

Sometimes a picture is worth a thousand words, so here is an example from a school where I used to be an Assistance Principle showing how to create mission, vision, and value statements.

I. Mission/Vision/ Values/ Goals

Part 1: Unpacking Your *Mission* Statement

Name of Organization: Jefferson High School "Inspiration Academy"

Mission Statement:

Merchants of Inspiration will experience the many facets of athletics, fitness, and health through interdisciplinary curricula, meta-cognitive development, and a student-centered approaches to inquiry-based learning for lifelong scholarship.

Based on the mission statement,

Who does the organization serve?

The Inspiration Academy serves students in grades 9 - 12 who are interested I sports and medicine careers.

What does the organization do for these people?

The organization provides exposure to careers and subjects that may lead to adult vocations. *What key values does the organization hold as it delivers this service?*

OUR VALUES: Merchants of Inspiration will be:

I*nquisitive*

*accou*N*table*

*hone*S*t*

*hel*P*ful*

*tenac*I*ous*

R*espectful*

*embr*A*cers of change*

T*eammates*

promoters of I*ntegrity*

*hard w*O*rkers*

*determi*N*ed to succeed*

Next, break the mission statement out into separate phrases. Each phrase should be a distinct promise made by the organization to its constituents. The mission statement may only have one promise or several. For each promise, list two or three pieces of evidence that the organization fulfills its mission. Also, for each promise, list two or three pieces of evidence that you wish the organization had to better fulfill its mission. Here is an example:

Phrase: **Merchants of Inspiration will experience the many facets of athletics, fitness, and health.**

Evidence You Have

- The pathways include sports medicine, sports management, physical education, and nursing. The courses are designed to expose students to each of these areas

- Students had the opportunity to select a small learning community based on their personal interests

Evidence You Need

- We do not have staff that can teach each and every course offered. We need a few more key teachers who can teach the subjects we choose to offer

Phrase: **Through interdisciplinary curricula, meta-cognitive development**

Evidence You Have

- Teachers are cooperatively developing lessons that meet standards across curricula
- As a small learning community (SLC), we meet twice a week to collaboratively discuss initiatives, data, instruction, students, and school process
- Students are taught through inquiry to expose misconceptions and find true understanding

Evidence You Need

- Staff and Administration need more training in delivering inquiry learning activities

Phrase: **and a student-centered approach to inquiry-based learning for lifelong scholarship**

Evidence You Have

- Students are taught through inquiry to expose misconceptions and find true understanding
- Students are exposed to specific areas of interest so they will take ownership of their learning

- Students are exposed to careers in the sports and medical fields, which might spark an interest and create a desire to pursue a future career
- A high percentage of students who graduate and attend college

Evidence You Need

- Students grades need to improve as a display of their investment in their education

Part 2: Unpacking Your Vision Statement.

1. Vision Statement:

All students will be *inspired* to seek intellectual growth and develop character. Together, we will pave the road to success.

2. Ideally, the vision statement reflects where an organization would like to be in 5 - 10 years. Elaborate more on these questions:

What is the dream reflected in the vision statement?

- That 100% of our students can and will be successful in their personal and educational lives.

By inference, what is the nightmare?

- The nightmare is that our failures will overshadow our success.

Break the vision statement out into separate phrases. Each phrase should be a distinct hope expressed by the organization to its constituents. The vision statement may only have one promise or several. For each hope, list two or three pieces of evidence that the organization is working toward this ideal. Also, for each hope, list two or three pieces of evidence that you wish the organization had to achieve this ideal.

Phrase: **All students will be *inspired***

Evidence You Have

- Small learning community meet twice a week to plan new innovative ideas and strategies
- Student success is regularly celebrated
- The SLC plans academic and social incentives

Evidence You Need

- Staff should design a survey that can assist us with an assessment of our students' motivation

Phrase: **to seek intellectual growth and develop character**

Evidence You Have

- The SLC posts and preaches our values to students on a daily basis
- Staff participates in professional development regularly to enhance their effectiveness
- Students learn through inquiry to expose misconceptions and find true understanding

Evidence You Need

For students to pass course work and score threes and fours on standardized test

Phrase: **Together, we will pave the road to success.**

Evidence You Have

- Staff regularly perform data analysis and use it inform and enhance instructional practices

- Staff are child-centered and demonstrate concern for students' personal and academic well-being by consistently making themselves available for extra help through SLC initiatives such as ZAP (Zeros Aren't Permitted).

Evidence You Need

- We need to find ways to motivate students to want success for themselves

Part 3: Telling a Story that Illustrates the Organization's Values

1. Values Statement:

OUR VALUES: Merchants of Inspiration will be:

Inquisitive
accou**N**table
hone**S**t
hel**P**ful
tenac**I**ous
Respectful
embr**A**cers of change
Teammates
promoters of **I**ntegrity
hard w**O**rkers
determi**N**ed to succeed

2. Tell a story that illustrates at least one of the organization's values (1-3 pages). It may be a story that shows that the value is not present in the organization. As I reflected as the SLC leader, I thought about how great the teachers were and how hard they worked to meet high expectations set for the students and themselves. I incorporated two short success stories provided by Inspiration Teachers:

Student names have been changed

Story 1:

Alright, I know this sounds crazy, but the most impressive success story that has been on my mind is Jim Mores. Jim is a student in Special Education classes who was formally in a self-contained classroom because he didn't function well in a larger classroom. Jim struggled the last two school years cycling in and out of suspension for behavior issues. I've seen a huge improvement in Jim this year. To my recollection, Jim has not been suspended at all this year. His grades are consistently improving in his classes because he has made a choice to graduate. This past marking period, Jim had great attendance, every assignment was handed in on time, and he had the highest average in the class. His behavior still needs some work, but the changes Jim has made are evident in his classroom performance. If Jim continues down this current path, he will have the opportunity to graduate. This story represents our values because it shows hard work, determination, and what can be accomplished when students and teachers embrace change. Jim and I were committed to his success.

Story 2:

One success story I have had this year occurred while using ZAP (Zeros Aren't Permitted) to help Wally Dachshund make up enough missing assignments to pass chemistry during first and second marking period. Wally has been a senior more than once but has the desire to earn his diploma. In the past, he has not been accountable for his actions. There were many times that he didn't attend class and didn't make the commitments necessary to earn all his credits or pass his exams. Now, Wally is showing up for class, and he stays after school every day to get extra help. I attribute this change to his new level of maturity and a constant effort and will of my staff and me not to give up on Wally. This story represents our values because it shows the student is finally accountable and tenacious in his pursuit to graduate while staff members are working as a team to help him reach his goals.

3. Based on the types of organizational stories, identify whether this story is an organizational myth, a hero story, a failure story, a war story, or a story of the future. Explain.

Both stories are stories that reflect the future. The students have made a change and have embraced that change from dysfunctional students to hard workers concerned about achieving a diploma. This story is about their future and how it became a lot brighter when they were inspired to achieve intellectual growth and good character.

Part 4: Are the Organization's Goals SMART?

1. Goal Statements: Fill in the table with no more than ten of the organization's goal statements. If there are numerous goals, concentrate on those that are closely related. For each goal listed, check off whether you think the goal is *specific* enough, contains information about whether *it can be measured*, whether it is truly *attainable* in the time provided, whether it is *realistic* (in your estimation) that the workforce will be willing and able to complete the goal, and ensure that there is a deadline for completion.

Goal Statement	Specific	Measurable	Attainable	Realistic	Timely
Academic Achievement: Foster academic success for all students through collaboration, individualized education, and inquiry-based learning in an effort to meet and surpass NYS standards during the 2007-2008 school year	Yes	Yes	Yes	Yes	Yes

Social Development: Develop a sense of SLC (small learning community) and school pride through student and staff participation in initiatives that support the Inspiration pathways during the 2007-2008 school year	Yes	Yes	Yes	Yes	Yes
Citizenship: Promote respect, responsibility, and accountability to encourage the development of positive and effective members of society by modeling integrity and celebrating success each quarter.	Yes	Yes	Yes	Yes	Yes

Part 5: Reflection on Mission/Vision/ Values/ Goals

Write a reflection (1 page or less)

Symbolically, Jefferson is represented by a blue and gold jaguar, but that does not define the organization. Recently, the small learning communities within the school were charged with creating their own mission, vision, logo, and slogan. Each SLC is in the process of defining itself by creating their own identity with staff, students, and its leader. It has been a powerful experience to watch a group of individuals form a team by uniting through a vision for the small learning community. In the Inspiration SLC, the branding process has begun and will continue until all individuals in this SLC believe the shared, newly created motto: *Success is Inspirational.* Staff members are starting to believe. The anticipated outcome is heading toward fruition. A staff member who has been teaching for twenty years said, "I can't believe it; you guys are getting me to volunteer to do things!" Ownership is being established, and staff feel they are part of something, that their opinions make a difference, and change is possible. Kouzes and Posner (2003) suggest that enabling others to act by the empowerment of a shared vision will create cohesiveness and inspire people to work towards common goals. In this case, the common goal is student success.

EFFECTIVE CLASSROOM LEADERSHIP

Educational leadership is the key factor in the success of learning communities. Leadership should be visionary; creating a shared vision and a positive environment that attracts and retains the best people. Strong educational leaders keep up to date on best practices. They are confident, energetic, enthusiastic, good communicators, and work to involve the entire team in the process of continuous improvement. Good leadership implies a responsibility to make every member of the organization a leader.

To have maximum impact on students, teachers must invest beyond subject knowledge. Do not get it confused, the knowledge of the subject is important, but a teacher's leadership and human qualities are more important. Therefore, I will highlight the leadership qualities that teachers need to possess to ensure that no child fails this year.

1. Deep and well-rooted understanding of the subject matter

At the heart of classroom leadership is a deep understanding of the subject being taught. For teachers to make meaningful impacts on students, they must have a superior understanding of their territory and must love it. There is no separating the two. Without enthusiasm for the subject taught, teachers cannot convey the material in ways that cause students to want to learn. Teachers who are passionate about their subject matter inspire students to be passionate about it, too.

2. Endearing Personality

Teaching is partly acting, and acting ability helps greatly. Thomas Edison said, "Genius is one percent **inspiration** and ninety-nine percent **perspiration**." Teachers can't be afraid of hard work. Good and effective teaching is as much about passion as it is about reason. It's about not only motivating students to learn, but teaching them how to learn, and doing it in a manner that is relevant, meaningful, and memorable. Good teaching is good leadership. It's about caring for your craft, having a passion for it, and conveying that passion to everyone, most importantly to your students. **A good teacher is warm, accessible, enthusiastic, and caring.** Good teachers are approachable, not only by students but everyone on campus. Students know which teachers are accessible and go to them when they have a problem or just want to share a funny story.

3. Willingness to continue personal development

If you are going train students to be consumers of knowledge, then you mustn't stop developing yourself. You have to stay current in your field, read widely inside and outside your area of expertise, and remain on the leading edge of technology. But most importantly, you need to be able to bridge the gap between theory and practice. Immerse yourself deeply in your chosen field, talk to, consult with, and assist practitioners, and liaise with their professional communities. **Good teachers have a love of learning** and inspire students with their passion for education and course material. They constantly renew themselves as professionals on their quests to provide students with the highest quality of education possible. Good teachers welcome new teaching strategies and opportunities to incorporate new technologies into lessons and are always willing to share what they've learned with colleagues.

4. Ability to maintain discipline

Without good discipline, nothing important can be achieved. A good teacher is someone pupils respect - and slightly fear if necessary. These teachers are completely in control of what's going on around them. Pupils know the teacher will notice if they are misbehaving or if their work is incomplete or copied from another child and will take action - punish the child, perhaps, or require the work be done again. But the best teachers are not necessarily disciplinarians. They are a velvet hand in an iron glove. Pupils come to know, over time, that they are warm and generous, but they are not to be messed with. Discipline is essential, especially in a multi-culturally and racially diverse classrooms where behaviors vary widely.

5. Ability to listen and give feedback

Effective teachers listen to students, ask questions for clarity, are responsive, and remember that each student and class is different. Each person's ideas and opinions are valued. Students feel safe to express their feelings and learn to respect and listen to others. Teachers who listen create welcoming learning environments for all students. Great teachers possess good listening skills and take time out of their way-too-busy schedules for anyone who needs them. If these teachers have a bad day, no one ever knows—they leave personal baggage outside the school doors. Great teachers understand the importance of eliciting responses and developing the oral communication skills in quiet students and push students to excel. At the same time, they are human, respect others, and remain professional at all times.

6. Flexibility

Good teachers don't get upset when there is an interruption to the schedule. Great teachers realize that the interruptions are as much as part of the schedule as the planned activities. Being flexible, fluid, experimental, and having the confidence to react and adjust to changing circumstances are all hallmarks of effective educators. It's about deviating from the course syllabus or lecture schedule easily when there is more and better learning elsewhere. **A great teacher can shift gears** and is flexible when a lesson isn't working. This teacher continually assesses learning and finds new ways to present material to make sure that every student understands the key concepts. Good teaching is about the creative balance between being an authoritarian leader and a pushover. Good teachers maintain a balance between these poles at all times, depending on the circumstances. They know where they need to be and when.

7. An amiable and entertaining teaching style

Whether you agree or not, good teaching is good stage acting. Your teaching style should be entertaining without necessarily losing substance. Classroom teaching is an art; it includes lots of drama and performance. It should entertain as well as add value. It is not about being locked with both hands glued to a podium or having your eyes fixated on a slide projector while you drone on. *Good teachers work the room and every student in it.* They realize that they are conductors, and the class is their orchestra. All students play different instruments with varying proficiencies. A teacher's job is to develop skills and make all those instruments come to life as a coherent whole to make beautiful music.

It is okay to be funny! It's often about making innocuous jokes, mostly at your own expense, to break the ice and allow students to learn in a more relaxed atmosphere where you, like them, are human with your own share of faults and shortcomings. If you are not naturally funny, don't bother about it. Just make sure your classroom environment is relaxing and full of positive learning outcomes.

8. Hard work

Teaching involves devotion, caring, nurturing, and developing minds and talents. It is no secret that teachers spend thankless hours grading papers, designing and redesigning course content, and inventing new ways to make learning fun and easy. It's about delivering a lesson with pace and interest, learning to use digital resources effectively, marking work and recording those marks, writing reports, teaching tricky concepts, asking questions of pupils in the most effective way, and giving extra time to children who need it. Good teaching is also highly-organized work. Teachers that don't want students to fail are passionate about their school and their pupils, keen for all to do well. They are highly organized because switching in a few seconds from one class to another, keeping track of individuals, remembering which extra duties they are down for, and managing record-keeping and databases requires coordinated effort.

9. High student expectations

Teachers should set high expectations for students because expectations greatly affect student performance. Expecting kids to do and perform well is a characteristic of all the best teachers. They try to ensure that every pupil masters the subject. This attitude sets the scene for everything that follows. Learning is hard work too, and some students never grow past mediocrity. They do the bare minimum required and little more. That's why as teachers, to ensure that no student fails this year, we must work tirelessly to create challenging, nurturing environments for our students. Students who produce unsatisfactory work must do it over until they succeed. Students must be tested regularly to see whether they have mastered the content, and those who do poorly should be provided opportunities to make corrections, to deepen their level of understanding, and to test again.

To ensure that no child fails this year, teachers must understand that the quality of teaching and the concerted effort of both the student and the teacher are what ensures excellence and high academic achievement.

10. Ability to create a sense of belonging and community

The mutual respect in a classroom provides a supportive and collaborative environment. In this small community, there are rules to follow and jobs to be done, and each student needs to be aware that he or she is an important, integral part of the group. Discipline and mutual respect must be maintained. Communicating dependability lets students know that they can rely not only on the teacher but also on the entire class. Provide opportunities to assume leadership roles in the class to further galvanize shared decision-making, teamwork, and community building.

11. Ability to collaborate with colleagues and mentors

Rather than thinking of herself as weak because she asked for suggestions or help, a good teacher views collaboration as a way to learn from fellow professionals. A great teacher uses constructive criticism and advice to grow as an educator. Good teaching involves mentoring between senior and junior faculty, teamwork, and being recognized and promoted by peers. Effective teaching should be rewarded, and poor teaching needs to be remediated through training and development programs.

To ensure that no student fails this year, teaching must be supported by strong and visionary leadership and tangible instructional support resources, personnel, and funds.

The kind of teaching that changes lives is continually reinforced by an overarching vision that transcends the entire organization, from the principal to teachers to part-time instructors, and is reflected in what is said, but more importantly by what is done.

12. Professionalism

To garner respect and to be taken seriously, a minimum level of professionalism—from personal appearance to organizational and communication skills—must be maintained. The respect that good teachers receive because of their professional manner is obvious to those around them and is important in driving home results.

Above all, the kind of teaching that changes lives is that which is fun where both students and teachers experience pleasure and intrinsic reward, like when locking eyes with a student in the back row and seeing the synapses and neurons connecting, thoughts being formed, the person becoming better, and a smile cracking across a face as learning all of a sudden happens. It's about the former student who says your course changed her life. It's about another telling you that your course was the best one they've ever taken.

SAFETY, SECURITY AND ACADEMIC DEVELOPMENT

A key contributor to the educational success of an average American student, particularly a Black male, is school safety. Without effective safety measures to mitigate gang violence, illegal firearms, and physical assault to mention a few, the plan of achieving high educational success rates in public schools will forever remain a pipe dream. This is because regardless of how good the teachers or the curriculum are, violence makes it difficult for students to learn. School violence takes many forms including gang activity, locker thefts, bullying and intimidation, gun use, assault, threats of force, arson, extortion, theft, hazing, bomb threats—just about anything that produces a victim. Violence is not only perpetrated against fellow students but also teachers and staff, and range from intentional vendettas to accidental killing bystanders.

Approximately three million crimes a year take place in or near our 85,000 public schools. Incidentally, student drawings of the perfect school often include police helicopters and security personnel. Available data shows that victimization rates are similar in junior high and high schools though they seem to peak among 13- and 14-year-olds (eighth and ninth graders). Overall crime rates are higher among students who have moved frequently, and rates seem to increase slightly as income increases (mainly because of increased property crimes).

Victimization rates seem to be largely independent of whether the student lives in a central city, suburb, or rural area. Still, the effect of school violence is broader than actual victimization statistics suggest. Violence is a problem in any societal setting. The problem is compounded when it involves schools because violent behavior and actions take away from the educational process. Violence affects student behavior. Kids act differently to avoid the threat of violence. Some students take a special route to get to school that often makes them late for classes because they are avoiding some form of victimization. Others stay away from certain places in the school or school playgrounds that would have improved their skills in extra-curricular activities and might have later in life give them a good shot at a college scholarship. Some stay away from certain school-related events that could have benefited them immensely; some deliberately stay in groups, and some stay home and ignore school totally and end up becoming a liability to society.

Students who spend their time thinking about violence and rearranging their lives to avoid violence are spending valuable mental effort that could otherwise be spent on learning or fun; they are foregoing the pleasure that they would have enjoyed by frequenting the places they now avoid.

Domestic violence and child abuse, which foster learning and behavior problems as well as frustration and retaliation, are also culpable in cases of school violence in America. Society-wide and juvenile violence eventually spills over into the school. In addition, the drug culture and its violent distribution networks encourage students to arm themselves.

Poverty lays the foundation for anger and discontent, and in many Black communities, issues of school violence can be expected to be high, as are communities that are plagued with illegitimacy and the breakdown of families. Kids have no place to feel safe, so they seek the stability and what they think is a caring environment of gangs and street life. Street life can make you feel like you have a support system of people who have similar struggles. Struggles, pressure, and stress make a bed of dysfunction for groups of like-minded individuals unless they all develop the mindset that they have to do better and change their circumstances. In cases where that happens, creativity and talents are cultivated and can change communities. By establishing safe schools, an avenue opens for students to be themselves and focus on education rather than postulating as someone they really are not or don't want to be. The cost of violence in society (i.e., purchases of security systems, carrying of guns, enrollment in self-defense classes, and avoidance of certain streets at certain times) is measured not only by actual harm, but by expenditures to avoid harm, and by the general disruption to people's lives. Despite the extraordinary media coverage of and public concern over violence in our schools, students are safer there than in any other place except their homes. Still, school officials recognize the potential threats to the safety of children attending school and school-related activities.

There is no one-size-fits-all solution to the problem of school violence. Many researchers have shown that there is no one program that could be a sort of silver bullet that when implemented will be effective for all schools. The ideal violence prevention policy is different from school to school because not all schools are the same in terms of crime rates in surrounding communities, quality of leadership, teacher quality and level of commitment, budgetary constraints, and other differences. However, some schools have dealt with the problem of guns in schools through punitive means (by suspending or expelling students for carrying a weapon), by heightening security (e.g., metal detectors), or by educating people on how to react to gun crime situations in such a way as to produce minimal bloodshed—for instance, training teachers on guns and violence (as in lockdown drills), and telling them what to do if a student pulls a gun in class (like don't make any fast moves and follow the student's orders, etc.).

Students are also taught mediation skills (problem solving and communication) and ways to handle their emotions—especially anger—without causing harm to others. These skills help them avoid potentially dangerous situations. Students are also being taught "safe" behaviors such as doing activities in groups, alerting school personnel if a stranger is on school property, and reporting situations that threaten the safety of other students.

The following provides an additional framework for planning and implementing a school safety plan that involves and empowers youth and adults in creating safer schools. Several of these tips provide opportunities for increasing student involvement and empowerment. Other keys are typically the responsibilities of teachers and other adults, so involving students in these areas will require strong youth development practice. The information provided below informs school leaders on how to create a safer school and achieve critical educational outcomes.

Establish A School-Community Partnership Coalition

Reducing incidents of bullying and violence requires a comprehensive, community-wide effort best coordinated by a school-community partnership. This partnership will generally include law enforcement, faith groups, businesses, government, community-based and youth-serving organizations, along with students, teachers, administrators, and parents.

Provide Alternatives to Gangs

School districts and communities should work together to offer students alternatives to gang membership, including activities that build self-esteem and help students deal with feelings of powerlessness. Some of these strategies might include providing special assistance to students who are at risk of gang membership, creating an environment that encourages a sense of belonging in all students, informing parents and school staff about gangs, teaching students how to avoid being drawn into these gangs, and giving students regular opportunities to discuss school experiences and to plan for future successes and rewards.

Improve School Designs and Physical Environment.

As school buildings are constructed and old ones are renovated, safety should now be an essential element of design. In new schools, office areas should be centrally located for easy access from other locations in the building or campus. Hallways should have convenient exits and be well lit at all times. Dead-end hallways and staircase hideaways should be eliminated, and restrooms should be located closer to administrators to prevent students from engaging in unsavory behavior such as smoking or bullying.

Every school needs to make sure that its students and staff are protected from the most likely potential threats – student weapons on campus, armed intruders, or other unwelcome visitors. However, new fencing, locks, cameras, and metal detectors are not the only way to make the physical environment safe. The overall quality of the physical environment has a significant impact on how students feel at school, which influences how they behave. Are the halls and common spaces sterile, or are they student-friendly, containing plants, student art, projects, and awards? Are grounds clean or littered? How quickly do you respond to graffiti or vandalism? How quickly are repairs made to broken items? The answer to these and other important questions are part of a general self-assessment about the physical environment that every school leader should conduct.

Monitoring Visitors Carefully

Schools need to assertive in screening visitors, requiring them to register when entering the campus, and employing security personnel. Schools can be both secure and friendly by requesting that visitors "check in" rather than "report to" the office. Registered visitors can be given a pass or badge to display prominently to let staff and students know that the administration has acknowledged them. Staff and students should be trained to report people without proper identification to a school administrator. Schools should now ask that parents give the names of adults who are allowed to pick up a child, and require those individuals to show identification to school personnel when signing out a student.

Set Clear Behavioral Standards, Policies, and Procedures

Every school or school district needs to review their disciplinary plans of action and set clear standards of behavior that are known and supported by all members of the school community. There should be clear consequences for those who violate these standards, and these consequences need to be implemented consistently. It is also important to note that a lot of schools are moving away from punitive discipline to restorative justice practices, as these are more effective in application and incur less cost financially. A school-wide code of conduct needs to be implemented that includes expectations, discipline and consequences, and positive rewards. The school-wide code of conduct should be collaboratively developed by all stakeholders and based on the needs of the school and the surrounding community.

Empower Students as Agents of Social Change

Schools are allies, partners, and vehicles of social change for school safety. As such, they need to enlist the help of an organized team of students—the socially influential opinion leaders of its diverse groups and cliques—who are committed to noticing hotspots and tipping points and trained to cool them off. Students have observation skills to notice such negative acts as exclusion, put-downs, teasing, relational aggression, bullying, harassment, and other forms of mistreatment that usually go unnoticed by adults. By training students in nonviolent communication and intervention skills, they can interact with their peers to prevent and stop bullying and harassment when and where it happens – on the bus, in the yard, at lunch, in the locker rooms and bathrooms, in the halls, and on the fields.

Implement Activities That Encourage Diversity

As school administrators, our school calendar should infuse the entire school with ongoing activities that promote tolerance, deepen understanding, and increase respect for differences. Activities will have greater impact when they are not stand-alone, but are consistent with themes woven into the educational curricula. These efforts will go a long way to decrease the tensions between the cliques and interest groups on the school campus. Through opportunities to learn about other people, assumptions, stereotypes, and prejudices are replaced with acceptance, tolerance, and compassion, thus reducing discipline incidents in the school.

Create Opportunities for the Least Engaged Youth

Many students feel disengaged and consequently feel left out. Dozens of studies have shown that students who lack a sense of belonging are at greater risk for acting out, or dropping out. Athletics, academics, and traditional activities do not always meet the developmental needs of all students. Therefore, it is necessary to create new and diverse opportunities for these least engaged youth to reconnect with their school and community. Initiate opportunities for dialogue and surveys that ask these students what they want to become involved in and how they want to become involved. Doing so will reduce the risk of them picking up an activity that may, in the end, bring harm to themselves or the school.

Support Social Skills Curricula and Instruction

Students benefit from the active teaching of the social-emotional skills that equip them to communicate effectively, establish solid friendships, and resolve their differences in nonviolent ways. This works especially for kids in elementary schools. Teachers can directly teach lessons on these skills, and learning can also happen more indirectly through class meetings and other strategies (like cooperative learning) that teachers can apply in their classrooms. Success requires that students experience consistent messages in all social-emotional curricula and all classes. It won't work as well if a handful of teachers spend twenty minutes a week on friendship skills while the others spend three hours and weave it into their activities for the week.

Conduct Professional Development Training

It doesn't matter the role whether classroom teachers or bus drivers, attendance secretaries or administrators, counselors or librarians, all adults have a role to play in building and maintaining a positive, healthy, and safe school environment. Unfortunately, professional development opportunities are few, and many adults haven't received the necessary training to be fully effective in understanding misdemeanors with far reaching consequences. Subjects like cyberbullying and relational aggression are complex, and most personnel do not have enough training to intervene effectively when they do notice the more pervasive forms of bullying, and some need to practice their "hall friendly" skills.

Many adults fail to utilize opportunities to build positive and long-lasting relationships with students beyond their classroom. These relationships not only improve the environment of the school and students' sense of connection to it, but they also become the pathways students use to inform authorities about fights, weapons, or other potential harm to people or property.

Encourage Increased Parent Involvement

Because parents significantly affect students' opinions, values, and interaction skills, parent understanding and support are essential for any school safety action plan to yield valuable success. We all know that open houses usually draw only the familiar faces of the highly engaged parents, so schools must find other ways to connect with other parents, especially those who are passively involved in the education of their children. Creating neighborhood meetings, hosting incentivized parent training, and educating more parents about the ever-changing nature of bullying will help in creating schools that are safer for learning.

XVI

IMPLEMENTING A RESULT-ORIENTED APPROACH TO EDUCATION

A result-oriented approach seeks to empower every individual so that they achieve their fullest potential. In other words, it is a holistic approach to education which transcends the regime of examination results and is focused on the total development of the individual that examination results cannot measure. The result-oriented approach to education is one of learner attributes relevant to the changing dynamics of knowledge societies. We must develop our perspectives concerning these attributes to ensure individuals will not fail in class or life.

1. Become a Self-Directed Learner

Today's learner is an autonomous learning individual and education can provide him with the right environment, guidance, and intervention to succeed. The learner should be endowed with the drive, zeal and skills to learn to learn. Education should be a continuous process of taking the learner from dependence to independence. It also means each learner is self-motivated. Schools should become learning labs where students and teachers experiment, innovate and learn from each other's experiences. It should be a place of intense activity where every member is valued and seeks new paths. In these learning laboratories, teamwork and problem solving are prioritized, and rather than assessing "instructional quality" in terms of coverage of content, "student's quality of learning" is assessed instead. In other words, teaching students takes priority over teaching content. Including structures such as Professional Learning Communities (PLC) with debate as well as collaboration can expand perspectives and help all to reach high levels of understanding.

2. Become an Efficient Knowledge Worker

In today's knowledge societies, the learner should be empowered not only to acquire knowledge but also to locate access, analyze, evaluate, and create knowledge. This requires education to provide the appropriate skills as well as the route map for transfer of skills so that the learner can apply them in real life to reap the benefits of learning. This necessitates technology integration at every level of learning and growing.

3. Become Entrepreneurial

The one attribute that has to be built up at a critical pace is the spirit of enterprise in our students. Schools need to be places where students learn to innovate, problem solve, and think critically. The ability to take manageable risks, perceive opportunities that can be developed into enterprises, innovate, lead from the front, become self-employed, and create jobs and wealth are crucial to the youngsters of a nation that are stepping into global competition. Compliance and obedience should stand far behind on the list of priorities when it comes to learning endeavors. Self-discipline and grit are more important than compliance and obedience.

Standardized tests to assess student success only demonstrates a fraction of the skills and attributes that contribute to a holistic education, and because these tests only measure a fraction of what's important with regard to success, they deserve only a fraction of the education efforts and dollars available.

Overprotecting and spoon feeding in the name of preparing learners for examinations kills their initiative and makes them accept stereotypes and status-quo. Many schools conduct too many examinations thereby stressing students and making learning dull and often painful. Rather than too many dull assessments, students should engage in ongoing, formative activities which include assessments to gauge their growth and academic needs. Also, too much competition dulls children's natural talents and abilities. Therefore, we have to keep a constant eye out to make sure that our focus is on student learning rather than doing better than the next school, state, or country.

4. Human and Social Development

In a world that is plagued by violence, a world that is generating increasing uncertainty about the future, education is what prepares students to face future challenges. The emergence of multi-culturalism has added a new dimension to the art of learning to live together. The social values of mutual respect, adaptability, cooperation, and coexistence should be harmonized with human values like empathy, kindness, and service, probity in public life and honesty in private dealings. Lastly, part of this development is making sure that students can see themselves within the curriculum you teach. Make sure that it is culturally relevant.

5. Culture

Besides getting in-depth knowledge about one's indigenous culture, the learner should accept and appreciate cultural diversity. Education should make the cultural roots stronger and nurture the global cultural branches.

6. Life-Long Learning

Societies thrive when their members strive to learn throughout their lives. The desire to learn can be kindled in school. As teachers, we get to foster in our students the "drive, zeal and skills to learn to learn." Education should be a continuous process of taking the learner from dependence to independence, and known to unknown. Education should make it clear to students that learning is neither confined to nor limited by institutions like schools, colleges, and universities. It is an ongoing process and if we want to continue to be successful; we must continue to learn. If all members of society were lifelong learners, we would have many less social ills and economic problems.

7. Passions and Interests Coupled with Emotional and Social Intelligence

Children exhibit keen interest and passions in many areas, and if we harness these interests and tie them to our curricula, we will have happy, productive kids willing and eager to learn. We need to acknowledge a child's social and emotional intelligence and grow and nurture them as children mature. They should be acknowledged and fostered appropriately in school environments. We need to make sure that our schools promote students' passions and interest with choice, consideration, cooperation, and collaboration rather than compulsion, comparison, and competition.

8. Ethics and Values

Mutual respect, adaptability, cooperation, and coexistence should be harmonized with human values like empathy, kindness, and service, probity in public life and honesty in private dealings.

The result-oriented approach embeds a strong academic foundation with positive mindsets, independence, and student passion and interests. It implies a focus on the intersection of processes including scheduling, roles, and structure prior to a focus on results. Streamlined, efficient, focused systems will allocate adequate time and attention for education's focal point: student learning. It is a different way of thinking, feeling, and acting.

Let me give you a realistic roadmap that will guide you in establishing a result-oriented approach.

Characteristics of Result-Oriented Leaders

- Energy: Energy is the scarce resource that brings plans to life. The leader's energy is the galvanizing force to get and keep the involvement of others.
- Personal Responsibility: Result-oriented leaders own the consequences of their own actions. They are excellent learners who can make corrections as needed.
- Focus on Results: Effective leaders are those who believe the outcome, not the process, is what matters most.
- Bias toward Action – Result-oriented leaders are actors, not critics, planners, or observers. They want to solve a problem, not bemoan, or even fully define it.
- Desire for Teamwork: School leaders are dependent on other people and forces for results. They enlist the full complement of "people power" to get the job done.
- Educational and Coaching Know-How: Successful leaders know and love what they do. They know what it takes to create learning and raise achievement.

A few time-management tips that might help

- Spending your time: You can tell a lot about a leader by where he or she spends time, in the schools and classrooms, or in the office. Where are you?
- Analyzing your time: To leverage your time toward achieving results, keep a log for a week on how you spend your time. In what ways is your leadership behavior increasing student success? Or not?
- Condensing time: Move off the problem and spend your time on the solution.
- Analysis to action. Start with the target and the results achieved (or not) so far, and then decide on the new action to make a greater difference.
- Handling meeting time: Shorten meetings, and focus every meeting on the results or product to be achieved, not the agenda.

Ways to create energy for success

- Motion - Action energizes. Just do it! Too much planning and analysis sap energy.
- Optimism - Enthusiasm, zest, and humor lift spirits, and create a can-do attitude. Be an energy generator.
- Urgency - Compressing time in pursuit of the target helps make behavior intentional to the result.
- Relationships - Personal connection and true praise make people take off. Toxic people are the greatest cause of loss of energy. Work with the early adopters and avoid the laggards.
- Spontaneity - The best new ideas and actions sometimes surprise. Encourage innovation. Reward the divergent.
- Success - Nothing builds energy like success. Affirmation, confidence. Recognize and celebrate success.

Tips on converting actionable data to results

Everyone has data, but where's the action to improve results? You've got to have the right kind of data -- frequent and common. Data points the way to action. For action to produce results, teams need to get organized and use the right techniques. One example of how to better use data to form action is to analyze the schools failures, which are the greatest indicator of student and teacher performance. I am including an example of a Quarter 1 analysis of failures, disaggregated by subject and grade individually, and then by grade and subject together. You will notice that the actual numbers of classes in each grade are broken out. There are seven periods a day because one period is lunch; times the number of ninth-grade classes are offered in totality. Do the same with each grade and subject in your school. Make sure to compare each year to the previous year. However, you must compare like quarters to get accurate data (Q1-14/15 school year to Q1-13/14 school year). You must do this for every quarter to get realistic, usable data that points in the direction your school is headed.

14-15 Q1 FAILURE INFORMATION

14-15 Q1 by Grade				
Grade	9	10	11	12
#Classes	786	596	547	360
#Failures	108	77	84	26
% of Classes	13.74%	12.92%	15.36%	7.22%

13-14 Q1 by Grade				
Grade	9	10	11	12
#Classes	792	691	549	347
#Failures	110	81	120	37
% of Classes	13.89%	11.72%	21.86%	10.66%

14-15 Q1 By Subject

Subject	ELA	Science	Math	Sst	Spanish	Other	PhysEd
#Classes	385	339	364	400	202	332	267
#Failures	31	74	73	34	31	44	8
% of Classes	8.1%	21.8%	20.1%	8.5%	15.3%	13.3%	3.0%

13-14 Q1 By Subject

Subject	ELA	Science	Math	Sst	Spanish	Other	PhysEd
#Classes	400	344	381	385	193	395	281
#Failures	37	83	80	34	17	77	20
% of Classes	9.3%	24.1%	21.0%	8.8%	8.8%	19.5%	7.1%

14-15 Q1 By Subject × Grade

	ELA	Science	Math	Sst	Spanish	Other	PhysEd
9	11	37	28	8	16	5	3
10	11	17	21	12	13	3	0
11	6	14	12	9	2	36	5
12	3	6	12	5	0	0	0

13-14 Q1 By Subject X Grade

	ELA	Science	Math	Sst	Spanish	Other	PhysEd
9	18	23	33	8	9	10	9
10	6	26	24	8	5	12	0
11	9	26	14	9	1	50	11
12	4	8	9	9	2	5	0

Once you have analyzed your failures, you can set goals and use the data in an actionable form which should be in line with your school's goals, mission, vision, and values. Some strategies to put the data in action are:

Identify Focus Students for Q2

- Based on the number of F's students earned in your department, you will be asked to pick a small number of "focus students."
- Pick students who failed in Q1, but who you think could pass in Q2.
- Encourage, motivate, engage
- DO NOT just pass them.
- The selection you make will not be used to evaluate you. It is entirely for your benefit, to help you focus your efforts and energy.
- Pick the students based on their numerical grade (grade average of 60-65%) and post their names somewhere you will consistently look, but others won't see, so will not judge the students.

Give teachers a small manageable amount of students to work with during the next quarter based on the target goal you set. We wanted a 10% reduction in failures, so we assigned based on five teachers per department.

- Science and Math – 3 students per teacher
- Spanish and Electives – 2 students per teacher
- ELA, SST, and PE – 1 student per teacher

Students on the Bubble

Monitor students who are not failing but are on the bubble of failing. If they have more than two D's, you may want to create an action item for them as well. Be proactive!

- There are some needy students who are not failing, so they may fly under the radar.
- While not a crisis, watch these students closely for signs that they are slipping
- 13-14 Q1 "Extra Bubbly" Students
  - 2 or more D's, but no F's, in quarter 1
  - 21 students who need to be monitored and supported

Goals:

Dept	# Teachers in the department	# Focus Students per Teacher	Goal for # of Failures in Q2	Goal for Percentage of Failures in Q2
ELA	5	1	26	6.8%
Science	5	3	59	17.4%
Math	5	3	58	15.9%
Sst	5	1	29	7.3%
Spanish	2	2	27	13.4%
Other	5	2	34	10.2%
PhysEd	3	1	5	1.9%

Personal Goals for GTH 2014-2015

The goal is for a 10% reduction in course failures compared to the previous year. Depending on what this means, we either achieved it with flying colors or failed abysmally. The question is, does the goal refer to a 10% reduction in the raw number of F's, a 10% reduction in the failure rate, or a 10-point reduction in the failure percentage? You have to figure out which one will provide the best data, and which is in line with your action plan.

- Number of F's: reduced by 15% (from 348 to 295)
- Failure rate: reduced by 12% (from 14.6 to 12.9)
- Failure rate: reduced by 1.7 points (from 14.6 to 12.9)

Monitor Student Progress

Have the teachers keep a log of the students and how the interventions are or aren't working. Communication amongst the staff about their targeted students keeps it fresh on their minds and provides opportunities for other teachers who have relationships with the students to add advice and expertise. Sometimes different people just know how to motivate certain students when others don't. If the interventions aren't working, take swift action and revise or change the action.

(Note: Names have been changed)

Duller	M. Michaels- still doing little to nothing in class, not coming to make up work … not sure how to motivate this young man, please advise.	K. Dole- attendance has been an issue and has not made up work, asked the parent intervention specialist to do a home visit.	E. Storm- not in school- can't help him unless we can get him here. The parent intervention specialist has started the PINS process.
Marcheno	B. Johnson is passing my class with 75. He completed assignments and participates in class more.	T. Stanley, his behavior is better, but he still failing with 62. He missed the last two assignments, but I am going to work to have him make them up.	
Jellon	C. Everest - he is coming to 1st period more often and changing his clothes and participating. Big difference from quarter 1.	P. Miley- he is coming to school and participating. He is also not missing as many days of school as he is my advisory student and he is doing well in all classes.	J. Chavez - Working harder to get grades up. Two classes are close to passing and on the rise while math remains the point of struggle. Staying after school for all classes and completing assignments now.

You can design the communication log any way you want; the important thing is that there are consistent communication and efforts to eliminate failures. Make sure the efforts are calculated and precise. Another key element to a successful result-based approach is to work effectively in teams.

The Teams - Get organized

Teams: Be clear on which are the best teams for your school to get the best results (by department, grade level, etc.).

Time: Make sure teams have time to meet for an hour at least every two weeks.

Facilitator: Provide a trained facilitator on each team who knows how to take data to action.

Purpose: Know what the purpose of the data meeting is - improved student performance, and what the non-purpose is - business as usual.

Norms: Set up guidelines for collaboration - everyone contributes.

Minutes: Provide one-page minutes and determine which data, what action, and how to reassess.

The Action - Use the right techniques

Data: Start with the team's frequent common assessment data.

Technique: Move from analysis to action and then assessment again.

Cycle: Recognize that the analysis, action, assessment cycle repeats through the year, with constant adjustment to find the most effective instructional action.

The Principal - Lead the Teams

Participate: When possible, participate in the data team meetings as an equal among colleagues.

Know: Know what's happening on your teams, through observation, conversations, and minutes.

Act: Act to strengthen weak teams, train facilitators, and provide professional development.

Adjust: Use key strategies to know where your school is and what key next steps will improve results.

REMOVE
ALL ZEROS
EFFECTIVELY
(RAZE-UP)

In too many schools across America rigor is defined as how difficult an assignment is. Does rigor have to be measured by difficulty, or should it be measured by how much an assignment provokes thought? Often rigor entails strict deadlines, deadlines which mirror colleges and universities. However, in my 15+ years of experience, I have learned that if you want to be successful, you have to meet children where they are at. K-12 education is about children, not adults. Adult's brains have developed enough to adhere to strict deadlines, with consequences for not meeting them. Some adults may say that we have to train the students through a black and white process, and they will learn from their success and failures. That's a bunch of bologna because education is not black or white, it is very gray. Gray enough that most students need programs and interventions customized for them and their success as individuals. Teachers may read this and roll their eyes, but I ask that if you just rolled your eyes, please stop and think for a moment if you learn more from failing with no support, or failing and having the opportunity to relearn the information based on what you didn't understand the first time around.

Children need time and support to develop, especially when they face daily adversity. That doesn't mean we make excuses for them or lower our standards, but it does mean that the traditional thought process of pass and fail needs to be revisited. Often urban children have so many distress factors in their lives that homework may not be a priority. They may not have slept, eaten, or had heat and hot water. If their basic needs are not met, how as educators can we expect children to follow the same guidelines as someone who has slept, eaten, and had heat and hot water? Going through a charter school renewal process, the Charter School Institute representative said to me that the school needed more built-in interventions to support students in need. I agreed because I found that in most urban schools, power and jurisdiction over students become very limited after dismissal. Having after-school programs is a great thing, but many students don't or can't stay after school, so they miss out on opportunities to get support.

As educators, we have to do things to level the playing fields in every way possible if we want to make sure kids succeed. Failure can no longer be an option. WE MUST DO BETTER. As educational leaders, teachers, parents, or community members, we have to make sure that the proper support systems are in place for our kids. Schools are a great place to begin.

I remember that one day years ago when these ideas all started to come together for me. I had a student named James who failed every quarter. The school year is usually divided into four quarters, and students earn a letter grade for each. The four letter grades get averaged at the end, and a final averaged grade determines if the student earns credit in a course or not. James went through ninth grade and did not earn enough credits to pass. Initially, I chalked it up to immaturity but thought he was competent enough to do it. The next year came, and he took some tenth-grade courses and the rest ninth, but instead of getting better, he got worse.

Failures became repetitive vicious cycles of despair. When he failed he became discouraged, disengaged, truant, and a downright pain in almost every teacher's ass. At the beginning of every quarter he would come in with a huge smile and say "Miller, I'm going to do better and pass this quarter. Watch and see." He would come in refreshed, reinvigorated because he felt like he had a fresh start at being successful. The first week went by, and he would come and show me his passing grades with pride. The second week, his grades would start to slip, and his smile decreased, his desire to be successful decreased and his pain-in-the-ass-ness increased. By week three, James was back to the cyclical pattern of failure. He always felt like he couldn't get caught up and there was no hope in even trying. Teachers would be discouraged and take the standpoint that if he only, would have, could have, should have, but he didn't. The fact that he didn't was made into James's problem and not the schools. How do you think that it all turned out for James and the school? I'll tell you…James dropped out of high school, and the school was closed down by the state due to poor performance. So what did that thought process get the school or James? Absolutely nothing, but shut down, dropped out, and another young Black man became a statistic. Something had to be done, and I knew I had to figure something out. I ended up taking a job in Albany, New York and although I was not able to make a difference for James, I vowed that I would make a difference for other young Black men who were just like James.

I created a program, loosely based on a program I witnessed in Tennessee on a previous professional development visit. I took what I learned back to my current building and collaboratively devised a way to make the program our own. The program is called RAZE UP. The RAZE stands for Remove All Zero's Effectively. It is an intervention which runs during the school day, and 100% of the school body can take advantage of the program. What the data has shown is that it can work for 100% of the student body, but year after year the data has shown that only about 62% take advantage of the intervention. The other 38% either don't do what they are supposed to, or fight against it and do nothing at all.

Of the 62% of students who actively participate, their grades have gone up an average of four points per week in each class. The interventions actually RAZED their grades up. Four points a week is statistically significant and has a huge impact on students' bottom lines. What RAZE UP does is create an opportunity to make sure that students cannot fail, will not fail, if they care just a tiny bit. James cared but didn't have a way to get caught up. What I have done in conjunction with a partner from the school, is create a system and software that assures students won't fail if the school can effectively roll out the system for them.

What is RAZE UP?

- RAZE is a period that occurs once a week
- We shave off 5 minutes from every class to create an extra period
- It is 9th period, and missing work, homework, test, quizzes, and content recovery are available to students
- RAZE is for students "Who Do NOT" take advantage of our after-school hours.
- Students get placed by the software in the course in which they have their lowest grade
- If the first option is full, they get RAZED to the second option
- Students with high grades get incentives and RAZED out

What is Not RAZE UP?

- RAZE is NOT a mandate (**Level 5?**)
- RAZE is NOT a study hall
- RAZE is NOT a disciplinary response to behavior
- RAZE is NOT a time for teachers to treat as a free period

Why is RAZE UP a GOOD idea?

- It will potentially increase student success on state Regents exams.
- It reaches the students who will NOT and do NOT stay after school.
- It can be used as Response to Intervention (RTI).
- It gives athletes an additional opportunity to maintain eligibility.

What potential assignments are given during RAZE UP?

- Make-up tests and quizzes
- Assignments which were not handed in
- Assignments which were not met with mastery
- Test corrections
- Alternative assignments for content recovery
- Additional enrichment work
- Online credit and content recovery

RAZE UP Summary

- Intervention Program for the ENTIRE SCHOOL
- Target students who do not stay after school, very differentiated
- Not a behavior intervention
- Not a free period for staff
- Award partial credit for assignments
- Monitor and use the data to inform results

CONCLUSION

This book began to materialize for me about 11 years ago when I was an Assistant Principal in the Rochester City School District. I was at one of the worst schools in New York State. The school was in one of the roughest neighborhoods in America. My hometown of Rochester is one of the poorest, most dangerous places in this country (murder capital of NYS), and where 9% of Black Males graduated in 2012. We were on the Persistently Dangerous list when I first arrived at the school. (For the record, I was able to devise new systems and protocols to get us removed from the Persistently Dangerous list). It was so bad that in my first month of school during Open House, which was held at night, a huge gang fight erupted outside at the bus stop in front of the school. One of the local gang members began to harass a student at the bus stop. The gang member punched the student in the face and tried to take his belongings.

The gang member had a few of his homies with him, and if the student had fought back, he would have gotten beaten up by all of them. Luckily, because it was Open House, adults were in the building, and several students were present at the bus stop. The students intervened and began to fight with the gang members. One of the students came to get me inside of the building. A security guard and I went outside to intervene. We were the only adults left in the building. It was complete chaos. It looked like a scene from a movie. Everyone was fighting and trying to hurt one another. When we got outside, we began to physically pick our students up and literally throw them inside the school. I believe I picked one young lady up with one arm and carried her in like a rag doll (I was in better shape then). We commanded them to remain inside while we went and removed the rest of our students from danger.

As I approached one of my students and instructed them to go inside, one of the gang members approached me, and it appeared as if he was thinking about what he should do. The look in his eyes was a deep stare of confusion on whether he should strike me or just flee the situation. I looked at him and stood my ground, preparing mentally and physically, as if I would have to defend myself against this 16-year-old. As I looked at him, I proclaimed that he should go ahead about his business and that he didn't want it with me. He chose to leave as I brought the last students inside to safety. It was then when I realized that it was going to take a lot more than just attempting to educate kids from 7:30 to 3:00 every day to assure that they did not become failures. It was going to take an extreme amount of care and trust to build rapport with the community and the students. That's not even mentioning what it was going to take to convince staff that we could make a difference.

I knew I had to do something to assure my students safety for the rest of the school year. Often students stayed late for athletic contests or other school-related functions. I knew that if I didn't intervene my students would be harassed regularly, and someone would get hurt. So I did some investigation and found out who was in charge of the gang and where I could find him. Freeman (my brother from another mother), another Assistant Principal and I went and had a conversation with the gang leader and some of the older members, who we ended up actually knowing. We both grew up in the city our whole lives and were not strangers to the streets and how they operated. So we approached in peace and asked for safe passage for our kids to and from school. We asked that he advise his young gunners (young members) that they leave our kids alone. In return, we vowed that we would not bring any police presence to his area. We assured that the school would not cause him and his area any problems. We didn't agree with how and what type of business was conducted, but we had to do what we had to do to keep our kids safe. Ultimately, we came to an agreement and students were not harassed anymore.

When I went to school for Educational Administration, they never said that negotiating with local gangs would be part of operating a school. Making sure that urban children succeed is so much more than instruction, tests, and homework. It takes a mindset that involves community, parents, school personnel, and a sincere desire by the student to do better. WE ALL HAVE TO DO BETTER! You don't need a formal education to get involved to keep youth from failing. You must look within and be willing to share your gifts and talents. Ultimately, I had to make a choice to go above and beyond to do everything in my power to assure the safety and well-being of my students, even though it was not in my job description. There are no job descriptions for saving lives. The youth are precious, and we have to do all we can to eliminate barriers to their success, whether it is in the community or the classroom.

This book was about discussing the issues and mandating that YOU, WE, I, All Do Better! YES, I AM YELLING AT YOU! We have to instill a new mindset in our youth and have to save them at all cost. We cannot allow them to fail in school anymore and definitely not in life. If they graduate high school their chances of being successful increase insurmountably. If students fail ninth grade, their chances of dropping out rise significantly.

This book touched on what various constituencies can do better to break certain cycles and change mindsets, but specifically focused on how the school can play a bigger and better part in assuring that all urban children succeed by not talking about best practice, but being about best practices. If you believe that students can make it and be something in life, please keep reading. If you're not willing to change your mindset, then STOP reading. Don't quit, just put this down and do some self-reflection and think about who helped you to make it to where you are today. Why are you successful? Most people did not make it to the top of the mountain without help along the way. You owe it to yourself, the community, and our youth to pay it forward. Okay, pick the book back up and keep reading because you are the difference maker. You have to believe it and have to act on it. Go to a school and volunteer, mentor, give time, money, and whatever is needed to make sure that our youth transform into the successful adults that I know they can be.

This whole book was about changing your mindset and doing things differently. Recently, I had a conversation with my amazingly smart and talented barber, Will, who is also a preacher. We discussed how much society needs to change. He stated that he preached a sermon recently, and how much in line it is with my book. He gave the example of how the criminal justice system is unfair. A White man and a Black man could commit the same crimes but get different sentences. When the sentence is applied, the community gets in an uproar and fights against it because of its unjust nature. When as a community are we going to stand up and fight against the behavior that caused the Black man to be in the predicament where he is facing unjust consequences? As communities, schools, and individuals, **We Must Do Better** and work towards improving our mindsets towards growth.

Every student can learn if they work hard enough is the initial thought that most people have, but we need more understanding of the emotional and psychological perspectives of our children. Ask yourself: Who is successful and why? What's the difference? Many times the difference is grit, passion, and perseverance for long-term goals. Staying with your future, Living life like a marathon, not a sprint is what Angela Duckworth said in her TED talk on GRIT. How do I build grit? Talent doesn't make you gritty. There are many talented individuals who don't follow through. However, Carol Dweck discusses in her work on the growth mindset that we must teach others the belief in their abilities to learn which can change with their own effort. The individual has to develop a "Don't Believe That Failure Is a Permanent Condition" attitude.

In order to create such an attitude, a few crucial steps need to occur:

1. Welcome challenge and challenge yourself (**Level 4?**)
2. Anticipate obstacles, show persistence and resilience
3. Greatness comes from effort; you get out what you put in

4. Learn to appreciate criticism and use it positively
5. Let others' success inspire you (Don't be a Hater or Teach Haterism).

Dweck and other speakers summarize by agreeing that you must teach the young urban youth to release their Fixed Amateur Mindset for a new Champion Mindset. A Fixed Mindset refers to the person who doesn't see beyond what is in front of them. Personal significance is attached to what's in front of them. A person with the fixed mindset is limited by where they are. The immediate gratification or lack thereof is led by what they see (media, etc.), versus what will come along with being mentally tough. Let's reverse the curse. The growth mindset belongs to the person who sees their bank account and sees opportunities when there are only a few dollars left. Growth mindset sees ultimate possibilities! The Champion - leans into their fear and shows up no matter how they feel. "Progression over Perfection."

The Champion focuses on what opportunities can be created. I once heard an example from a motivational YouTube clip that discussed the $600.00 versus $6,000.00 website. Someone with a Champion mindset who doesn't have the funds for the $6,000.00 website will take the time to think, problem solve, see the opportunity, and weigh which one will yield the greatest return for their business. They realize the $6,000.00 website will be more beneficial than the other and will find a way to either afford the $6,000.00 website or do everything in their power to make the $600.00 website function equally if not better. The Champion is mentally tough, and failure is not an option. They would never just settle. We have to teach our youth that failure is settling and that it can't be an option for them anymore. Go and ask better questions, ask your students if they're in a growth mindset, what's the outcome they want? What are they willing to do to achieve it? There is much we have to do to ensure that WE DO BETTER and change the future of our youth.

The success of every child in school, and by extension in today's society, depends on a variety of important factors including socioeconomic status, the intensity of care and emotional support that the child receives from the parent, the quality of learning and educational aid that the child receives from the school, the race to which the child belongs, and the mindset of such a child to succeed.

All stakeholders—parents, schools, communities, have important roles to play in ensuring that the mindset of failure in every school child is repressed, and failure in school is squashed totally. It is only through concerted efforts that this lofty ideal which is essential for the breeding of a generation of young, successful future leaders (particularly those who are ethnically-disadvantaged) can be achieved.

To advance our society on educational fronts so that no child fails, teachers have a lot of work to do. You are a teacher even if you are not in the educational sector. We are all at the forefront of the battle against failure. We are the direct injectors of formulations and executors of educational policies that in one way or the other set up our children for success or failure. In their formative years, most children spend a lot more time in school (with their teachers) than they actually do with their parents. Therefore, the experience they have with us goes a long way in determining their approach to education, their performance in school, and by extension their attitude toward success. We are the potters, effectively molding minds into what they should be. Every child deserves an opportunity to be successful, and it is our job as teachers and humans to do what we can, even going beyond our job descriptions to ensure that our young people do not waste away.

To create a successful system where no child fails, teachers must learn not to focus all attention and shower all encomiums on the high-achieving students alone. The shy and timid girl who avoids questions and the tattooed and disengaged boy who plays truant both deserve our help irrespective of their social class, family background, character tendencies, and intelligence level. Teachers should also learn to consistently fine-tune teaching methods and practices the suit trends. Students' interests such as sports, music, and social media should be considered for their potential tie to classroom materials.

School leaders must put in place systems, infrastructures, and practices that make schools safe and attractive so students will want to attend.

Parents must understand that they have a moral, social, and legal responsibility to their child. They are directly responsible for whatever a child turns out to be in life because they are the ones who decide the kind of parenting, welfare, and economic conditions needed to ensure that their child doesn't fail. Helping children take responsibility for their actions is a big step in the right direction. For example, when an incident happens with your child on the bus, admit when your child is wrong and work with your child and the school to make it right. No more sticking up for negative behaviors. Placing blame on the school instead of the child will not work anymore.

It doesn't take a neurosurgeon to figure out that unstable or broken homes are huge contributors to failure in children. Therefore, parents should display the right attitude, provide the required emotional and mental conditioning, and, of course, financial support to help their children succeed.

A lot has been discussed about the distorted illusion of immediate gratification and unbounded pleasure and material gain that the entertainment world fabricates in the minds of young people. It is the parents' duty to sanitize the minds of children by providing sound advice and counseling. Teachers also have a role to play in this.

Parents must collaborate with teachers on all fronts to provide a safe and secure school that fosters learning and development. The development of every child requires concerted effort; therefore, parents must follow up on their children educationally to fill up learning cracks. Stop just dropping the kids off and expecting the school will take it from there. Parents and schools have to develop a united front to see progress.

Parents and teachers must communicate and give feedback on improving grades, increasing interest in learning, reducing truancy, and eliminating emotional detachment, etc.

Lastly, financial support is important in building an effective citadel of learning. Parents should encourage the schools and teachers by making financial and material donations that would help make schools run more efficiently.

WE CAN DO BETTER! LET'S DO IT NOW!

REFERENCES

Abbott, S., & Freeth, D. (2008). Social capital and health: Starting to make sense of the role of generalized trust and reciprocity. *Journal of Health Psychology* 13(7): 874-883

Annie E. Casey Foundation, Department of Education National Center for Education Statistics. (2014). Retrieved from http://www.aecf.org/

Anderson, E. (1999). *Code of the streets.* New York: W.W Norton and Company.

Bandura, A. (1965). Influence of models' reinforcement contingencies on the acquisition of imitative responses. *Journal of Personality and Social Psychology, Vol. 1,* pp. 589-595

Barton, P. E. (2004). Why does the gap persist? Educational Leadership, 62 (3), 8–13.

Bennet-Johnson, E. (2004). The Root of School Violence: Cause and recommendations for a plan of action. *College Student Journal, 38*(2), 199-202

Burell, N. A., Zirbel, C. S., & Allen, M. (2003). Evaluating peer mediation outcomes in educational settings: A meta-analytic review. *Conflict Resolution Quarterly, 21,* 7 26

Currie, J., & Yelowitz, A. (1999). Are Public Housing Projects Good For Kids? Los Angeles, CA: University of California and National Bureau of Economic Research.

Danziger, S., & Haveman, R. H. (2001). Understanding poverty. New York: Russell Sage Foundation.

Dweck, C. (2007). *Mindset: The New Psychology of Success.* Ballantine Books.

Gonick, M. (2004). The mean girl crisis: Problematizing representations of girl's friendships. *Feminism and Psychology, 14*, 395-400

Greitemeyer, T. (2009). Effects of Songs with Prosocial Lyrics on Prosocial Behavior: Further Evidence and a Mediating Mechanism (as cited in Miller, 2012).

Home – Black lives matter. (n.d.). Retrieved February 12, 2016, from http://blackboysreport.org/

Jones, J. (1985). Labor of Love, Labor of Sorrow: Black Women, Work and the Family from Slavery to the Present, 113.

Jones, N. (2004). Girls fight: Negotiating conflict and violence in distressed inner-city neighborhoods. *Dissertations Abstracts International,* 1-237. (UMI No. 3138034)

Kerman, S., Kimball, T., & Martin, M. (1980). *Teacher expectations and student achievement.* Bloomington, IN: Phi Delta Kappa

Kiecolt-Glaser, J. K., & Newton, T. L. (2001). Marriage and health: His and hers. Psychological Bulletin, 127, 472-503

Kozol, J. (1992). Savage inequalities: Children in America's schools. New York: Harper-Collins.

Morrow, A. (2003). Breaking the curse of Willie Lynch: The science of slave psychology. Rising Sun Publications.

McLanahan, S. S. & Casper, L. (1995). Growing diversity and inequality in the American family. In *State of the Union: America in the 1900s.* New York: Russell Sage. Media Violence. (2001). *Pediatrics, 108(5),* 1222-1226.

NAACP, (2011).

Peter Fischer & Tobias Greitemeyer (2006). Music and Aggression: The Impact of Sexual Aggressive Song Lyrics on Aggression-Related Thoughts, Emotions, and Behavior toward the Same and the Opposite Sex

Positioning Young Black Boys for Educational Success. (2011, Fall). Policy Notes Fall 2011 News From the ETS Policy Information Center, 19(3), 1-15. Richard, R., Deci, M., & Edward, L. (2000). Self-determination theory and the facilitation of intrinsic motivation, social development, and well-being. *American Psychologist, 55,* 68-78.

Rindfuss R.R. & VandenHeuvel A (1990). Cohabitation: A Precursor to Marriage or an Alternative to Being Single? *Population and Development Review, Dec.1990, 703-26*

Santelli, John S. 2002. The association of sexual behaviors with socioeconomic status, family structure, and race/ethnicity among U.S. adolescents, *American Journal of Public Health, 90,* 1582-1588.

Schwartz, M. A., & Scott, B. M. (2003). *Marriages and Families: Diversity and Change (4th ed.).* Upper Saddle River, NJ: Pearson Education, Inc.

Segal, L. (2005). Battling Corruption in America's Public Schools. Cambridge, MA: Harvard University Press.

Seligman, M. E. (1975). Helplessness: On Depression, Development, and Death. San Francisco: W. H. Freeman.

Sutherland, K.S., & Singh, N.N. (2004). Learned Helplessness and Students with Emotional or Behavioral Disorders: Deprivation in the Classroom. *Behavioral Disorders, 29(2)*, 169-181.

Sunburst Visual Media (2003). *How not to be a victim: Violence Prevention.* Retrieved January 16, 2012, from http://www.ecb.org/guides/pdf/CE_68_06.pdf

Tolson, E. R., McDonald, S., & Moriarty, A. (1990). *Peer mediation among high school students: A test of effectiveness* (University of Illinois). Chicago: University of Illinois, Jane Addams School of Social Work.

Too important to fail. (n.d.). Retrieved February 12, 2016, from (n.d.). Retrieved from http://www.pbs.org/wnet/tavissmiley/tsr/too-important-to-fail/fact-sheetoutcomes-for-young-black-men/.

U.S. Census Bureau, 1996. Households and families. *U.S. Census Bureau,* Washington, D.C.

U.S. Census Bureau, 1992. Households and families. *U.S. Census Bureau,* Washington, D.C.